DATING,
RELATING,
WAITING

DATING, RELATING, WAITING

God's Word on Purity

Michael Ross & Tess Cox

An Imprint of Barbour Publishing, Inc.

Member of the
Evangelical Christian
Publishers Association

CONTENTS

START HERE

Sexual Attraction and Romantic Love—
It's All God's Idea!

So Why Not Follow the Right Plan?

One minute I (Michael) am flipping through channels on my TV—looking for something decent to watch—and the next minute I'm seriously confused.

What I'm seeing can't be real! I tell myself. *It's got to be staged. But why? Who would want to pretend to live this way?*

I've stumbled upon a popular "shock TV" show often viewed by teens. Today's topic: "Transvestite Gay Males and Their Female Lovers."

The host is interviewing a homosexual young man named Charlie who is dressed like a girl and a girl named Sarah who is dressed like a boy. Both claim to be lovers. Suddenly the girl pulls an engagement ring out of her jacket pocket and kneels in front of the boy.

"Charlie, we've been friends through high school," she says, "and you know how I feel about you."

The boy blushes, and the audience cheers.

"I want to spend my life with you," Sarah tells Charlie, offering him the ring. "I want to have your children. That's why I'm asking you to marry me."

The audience roars even louder. Even the host begins to pressure him. "So, what's your answer, Charlie?" the TV personality says. "She obviously loves you. Are you going to say no to this beautiful young lady?"

"But I'm gay," Charlie responds.

"I don't care," his lover says. "I think we can have a good life together."

After a long pause—the audience still cheering—Charlie looks at the host and says, "Yes, I'll marry her. But only because I love that gorgeous ring!"

As crazy as this story sounds, it underscores the broken sexual climate you are growing up in, not to mention today's casual attitudes toward sex, love, and marriage.

True, Charlie and Sarah represent an extreme case, and more than likely they staged their relationship—just for fifteen minutes of fame. (What do you expect from reality TV, right?) Yet a constant bombardment of mixed-up media messages coupled with bad influences from friends are taking a toll on your generation.

"I'm not one of those all-media-is-Satan kind of guys," says popular youth speaker and author Justin Lookadoo. "But in the case of sex and romance, it may be true. Do you know how hard it is to find a DVD, CD, or magazine without a bunch of skin-flashin' and sex-talkin'? It's like, that's all there is."[1]

A friend of mine—contemporary Christian music artist Josh Brown—agrees. "Today's teens are drowning in twisted sexual content from movies, TV, music, and the Internet," he says. "It's warping their view of love and relationships. I know this from experience: I came out of the secular music world. I've been there, and I see it happening to teens everywhere." (Josh started a band several years back called Day of Fire.)

When it comes to matters of the heart, even church-going teens are caving into what's popular—instead of what God's Word tells us is right:

Robert, 16, Durham, North Carolina: "Sometimes 'hooking up' with the opposite sex is just about fun, about recreation, not romance. My girlfriend and I really like each other, and it has come to the point where she and I want to kiss and stuff. But some of my friends say it's wrong in God's eyes to make out. To us, it's not a big deal."

Allie, 17, Augusta, Georgia: "If two unmarried people are having sex in a committed relationship, what should stop them? As a Christian, I've always been taught that premarital sex is wrong, but the problem is, I can't find scripture that says this specifically. Why do Christians create so many rules for something that everybody is doing?"

Josh, 16, Beaverton, Oregon: "I met a girl at camp who has all the qualities I'm looking for—including a strong faith in God. Even though we only spent a week together, I'm convinced that I've found my soul mate. But my parents believe otherwise. They say we're way too young to get serious romantically, especially to think about marriage. Our feelings are real, so what makes us too immature?"

Why didn't God make the quest for purity easier for teens? Why didn't He give you sexual desires on your wedding night. . .and not a moment before?

Could it be that our Creator wants to take you on a journey into *authentic* manhood and womanhood? I think so. I'm convinced that He wants to embrace that sometimes confused, sometimes awkward—but absolutely amazing—kid you see in the mirror and transform you into a young man or young woman fit to wear His badge: "a workman approved by God" (2 Timothy 2:15).

This transformation, like anything worthwhile in life, involves struggle.

Face it: Next to committing your life to Jesus Christ, setting godly standards for relationships and choosing the path of purity are two of the wisest choices you will ever make. So before you even think about dating, you must examine your motives. You must take an honest look at how you view love, sex, and marriage. Do you seek answers from the Bible, or are you going along with what the world says is okay?

"As a teen, I made many mistakes as I dated," says Josh (Day of Fire). "I've seen how immorality can destroy relationships and cause emotional, physical, and spiritual damage. Here's what I've learned: for any relationship to be successful, Jesus must be first."

This book can help. On the pages that follow, we'll show you how to. . .

- navigate sexual land mines
- take to heart what the Bible says about relationships
- communicate better with the opposite sex
- clue in to how guys and girls are wired
- plan the perfect date
- view purity as a lifestyle, not just a "line" to avoid
- find God's design for dating, relating, and waiting

CHAPTER 1

What's Your DQ (Dating Quotient)?

Take Our Quiz to Discover Your Dating Intelligence

D o you know your DQ? Just as your IQ (intelligence quotient) is supposed to tell how smart you are, your DQ measures what you know about dating, relating, and waiting. It's your dating intelligence quotient, and it's a pretty good predictor of (1) your romantic success in the months and years ahead, and (2) whether you need more "wait training" before you get started.

What's that—never heard of your DQ? Neither had we until we made it up! But it's time to find out what yours is, so just take your best shot at the questions below, and then tally your score. And don't worry. If your initial number is pretty low, we've filled this book with tips and strategies to help you raise your DQ.

Here's how this works: In the paragraphs that follow, you'll find eight gender-specific scenarios (guys are odd, girls even), as well as two more that are designed for both sexes. Read the appropriate stories, choose your answers from the multiple choice lists, add up your scores (there will be a total of six responses per quiz taker). . .and then discover where you land on the Dating-Relating-Waiting Scale.

Let's get started.

DQ Guys #1—Talking to Girls

Jasmine is cute, popular, and smiles a lot—mostly at you. *It's time to talk to her,* you tell yourself, *but how? And what should I say?* Every time you take a step toward her, your knees go weak and your stomach turns into a human trampoline. Even worse, your brain goes blank. But you decide to make a move anyway, so you breathe deeply and then. . .

A. tighten your muscles, lower your voice several octaves, and ask her if she likes what she sees.

B. blurt, "Whazup, girlfriend?" At that point, you break into your best rendition of "Stay with Me" by Sam Smith.

C. go to her locker and say hi, then walk her to class and ask questions that help you get to know her a little better.

DQ Girls #2—Getting His Attention

Your sophomore year of high school has brought a lot of cool surprises into your life, including a blond-haired, blue-eyed basketball player named Chris. He's smart, funny, and isn't afraid to take a stand for what he believes. You've spotted him recently at your school's Wednesday morning prayer club. For you, the attraction is instant, but how can you figure out if he's Mr. Right? You need to get his attention, so one morning you make a bold move and. . .

A. walk up to him in your super-tight blouse and crazy, skinny shorts. You cock your head sideways and wink.

B. slip a letter to your best friend's cousin's sister who promises to deliver it directly to Chris's third-period lab partner's brother, whose reputation for having stealthy ninja skills was well earned after he snuck a hundred notes into other people's backpacks last semester— which he can easily do to Chris's right now! (Catch all of that? *Whew*—more than a little confusing!)

C. grab a couple of friends, walk up to him, and introduce yourself. "Hi," you tell Chris, "we're so glad you've joined the prayer group." After sharing the names of your entourage, you then ask if you and your friends can sit by him, which will give you a chance to connect.

DQ Guys #3—Being Dateless

You're a few months away from turning eighteen, and you've never had a girlfriend, never been kissed. . .nothing romantic! And you're starting to ask yourself some hard questions: *Am I normal? Am I a loser with the opposite sex, or is it okay to be dateless?* You went to a Christmas dance with a girl several months back, and the two of you have gone out a few times. She's definitely a friend but not a *girlfriend*. It's the same with other girls in your life—smiles, laughs, and good times but nothing exclusive. Essentially, you're alone. *Lord, this feels like a cruel joke. Shouldn't I have a girlfriend, like all my friends? Am I weird? Did You somehow make a mistake with my romantic life?* One evening after a serious quiet time with Jesus, you decide it's time to settle this issue. You decide to face your dilemma and. . .

A. pop some breath mints, put on some lip balm, and plant a big, wet kiss on the first *girl* friend you meet!

B. plan the ultimate romantic date that's sure to turn one of your *girl* friends into a girlfriend.

C. stop believing that being girl-less means being less of a guy, and start letting God define your self-worth. Believe that despite what some of your friends are doing, it's okay not to have a steady girlfriend. *I can't force something just to fit in. I need to trust God's timing and His best for me.*

DQ Girls #4—Going Too Fast Too Soon

Lately those perfect romantic kisses that end a date have turned into making out every day after school. . .with much more touching—from hand to face, to shoulder and beyond. You quickly pull away, prompting him to stare back at you with those amazing eyes and ask, "What's wrong? Did I do something you don't like?" His words seem to hang in the air. You sit up, swallow, and say. . .

A. "Nothing. My bad—let's keep goin'."

B. "Thought I heard the doorbell. Better check it." At that point, you grab your cell phone and head downstairs. You frantically begin texting your best friend, begging her for advice.

C. "No. I like it too much and don't want to stop—and *that's* the problem. This is headed in one direction, but we can't go there. We both made a promise to be pure, so let's slow down."

DQ Guys #5—Cluing in to a Girl's Feelings[1]

Jada is a great friend. You hang out a lot, and you even text each other several times a week. So the other day at Taco Bell she starts asking if you think all these other girls in the restaurant are good-looking. *Okay—whatever,* you tell yourself. But then she says, "Do you think I'm pretty?"

After you choke on your Dorito Supreme, you. . .

A. ignore her question and begin shouting, "Ohhh, la chica!" every time a girl walks past your table.

B. answer, "Ummm, well, you're okay, I guess. Are you going to eat the rest of the chips and salsa?"

C. tell her, "Yeah, of course—but it's really awesome that you're not caught up in appearance all the time and act shallow like some girls. What I really like is that you're comfortable just being *you*. . .and letting me be *me*."

DQ Girls #6—Cluing in to a Guy's Feelings

You've been dating Ethan for more than three months, and for the first time, he's starting to share some of his deepest feelings: "It's as if we're supposed to be 'cool clones,' and I'm sick of it," Ethan tells you as he takes a sip of Coke. "I look around school and youth group, and all I see are cliques: the so-called 'cool kids' only hanging out with other 'cool clones.' And if you don't measure up, life is hell. Honestly, I'm tired of the pressure." You never realized Ethan felt this way—which is exactly how you feel sometimes. But you also know that the "cool clones" he described are the two of you, and it's a status you sort of like. *Who doesn't want to be accepted by the popular kids?* Still,

Ethan is sharing how he really feels inside, and you love that he's opening up. So what should you say? You pause then look him in the eye and. . .

A. defend your popularity, warning him, "Don't ever breathe those words to another soul. It will be our little secret."

B. avoid the subject altogether and ask if he'd like another Coke or if he'd like to take a break and head to the mall—anything to lighten the mood.

C. affirm his feelings. "I hate the pressure, too," you tell him, "and how cruel people can be if you don't fit in. I'm so glad you shared this, because I feel the same way. It's lousy to be rejected. We should all try to make friends with lots of different people, not just cliques. Let's help each other to be this way, okay?"

DQ Guys #7—Divine Dating Secrets

Your youth pastor is challenging everyone to put God first in *every* relationship—especially the guy-girl, romantic kind. "Here's what sets us apart," the pastor says. "Christ-following singles have learned to love the way Jesus loves. They've learned that real love is sacrificial, serving, and giving, and involves laying down our lives for someone else—not putting our own desires first.

Christ-following teens and young adults keep Jesus right at the center of every date, honoring Him and sharing Him through words and actions." The pastor has your attention, but you can't help but wonder if bringing God on every date would make things awkward. You slump back in your chair and tell yourself. . .

A. *girls would think I'm weird if I talked about Jesus every time we went out. I'll stick with the separation of "church and date."*

B. *nice in theory, but it's not what happens in the real world—even for Christian teens.*

C. *God is the foundation of everything—including my dating life. If purity is a priority to me, and if I want to live radically for Him, then I need to live my faith 24/7. I can't separate my dating life from my walk with Christ.*

DQ Girls #8—Handling Convertible Christians

You're well aware that lots of things in life are convertible—cars, clothing, computers, cooking utensils. But Christians, too? These types of believers act one way at church and at home, and then transform into completely different people when they're with the crowd. (And you're starting to realize that one of them is your closest friend.) You're on a spring break ski trip with your youth group, and a bunch of teens are spending more time sneaking away with each other. . .and less time on the slopes. "Come on," your friend says. "A couple of college guys are letting us hang out in their condo. Nobody's getting hurt; we're just having a little party." You pause for a moment. *This is my best friend,* you tell yourself. *Maybe I've been too quick to judge. Maybe I need to keep an eye on her.* You smile and. . .

A. compromise, saying, "I'll join you. . .but my finger is on our youth pastor's cell number just in case things go bad."

B. escape, saying, "I promised the others that I'd join them for lunch. Maybe later."

C. lead, saying, "Are you crazy? Partying with boys in a condo that two college guys are letting you use? That's not innocent; that's insane! You need to stay as far away from that place as possible. Come skiing with me."

DQ Both Guys and Girls #9—Everything but "It"

If sex is off-limits until marriage, what comes before *sex and marriage? Touching? Masturbation? Oral sex? Everything except intercourse? How far is too far? What's okay, and what isn't?* The questions swirl around your head. . .yet clear answers seem evasive. Your parents tell you one thing, the media says something else—and your friends seem just as confused as you. Who should you listen to? Where can you find trustworthy advice? Eventually your search comes to an end. *The one place I can go for answers is. . .*

A. *my media role models.* So many of them are rich, successful, attractive, smart, fulfilled, happy, and worth emulating. Just read your favorite entertainment guide for proof. (On second thought, maybe we should scratch this response!)

B. *my heart, and what I perceive as* right *and* wrong. After all, don't your own feelings and emotions have *your* best interests in mind? Aren't *you* the captain of your ship? Why shouldn't you do what feels right to you?

C. *my Bible.* While God's Word doesn't always give us specific details precisely the way we'd like them—"Do this but not that"—the Lord does give us broad principles to live by when it comes to sex and relationships: Sex is designed for marriage, lust is wrong, we are to be pure in our attitudes and our actions. Here are some verses to take to heart: Exodus 20:14; Matthew 15:19; 19:6; Romans 12:9–10; 1 Corinthians 6:12–20; Ephesians 5:3; 5:25–33; 1 Thessalonians 4:3–8; 1 Timothy 5:1–2; Hebrews 13:4.

DQ Both Guys and Girls #10—When Two People Are in Love

A friend of yours just returned from church camp walking on clouds. He met a girl who has all the qualities he's looking for—including a strong faith in God. Even though they only spent a week together, he's convinced that he has found his soul mate. And even though the two of them are only sixteen, they both think they are ready to get married. Your friend even confessed something to you: "Since we're in love and have promised to get married, we don't see anything wrong with having sex. If two people are willing to commit their lives to each other, then what should stop them?" He looks to you for some moral support. You fidget, clear your throat, and say. . .

A. "Love and commitment makes all the difference. It's like you're already married, so it seems okay."

B. "Turn or burn, dude! You and your girlfriend just bought a one-way ticket to hell—that is, if you don't repent." You then recite a bunch of Bible verses.

C. "Not having a wedding ring—that's what should stop you. Even though you *want* to get married and you *feel* married. . .the fact is, you *aren't*. And there's a good reason why God tells us to wait until *after* we're married to have sex. He loves us too much to let us do something we might regret. My advice: cool things down, spend some time in prayer, and talk to your mom and dad."

It's Time to Grade Your Quiz

DQ Guys #1: A = 7, B = 10, C = 27
My Response: ____ My Score: ____

DQ Girls #2: A = 7, B = 10, C = 27
My Response: ____ My Score: ____

DQ Guys #3: A = -7, B = 17, C = 27
My Response: ____ My Score: ____

DQ Girls #4: A = -7, B = 17, C = 27
My Response: ____ My Score: ____

DQ Guys #5: A = 7, B = 8, C = 27
My Response: ____ My Score: ____

DQ Girls #6: A = 7, B = 8, C = 27
My Response: ____ My Score: ____

DQ Guys #7: A = 3, B = 13, C = 27

My Response: ___ My Score: ___
DQ Girls #8: A = 3, B = 13, C = 27
My Response: ___ My Score: ___

DQ Both Guys and Girls #9: A = -3, B = 9, C = 27
My Response: ___ My Score: ___

DQ Both Guys and Girls #10: A = -7, B = 11, C = 27
My Response: ___ My Score: ___

TALLIED FINAL SCORE: ___

Dating-Relating-Waiting Scale

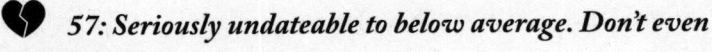 ***57: Seriously undateable to below average. Don't even think about dating. . .yet.***

Okay—you have some homework to do before you start a relationship with someone. In addition to reading this book from cover to cover (twice), we suggest you concentrate on these chapters:

Chapter 2: Getting Ready for the Dating-Relating Thing

Chapter 8: The Impact of Sexual Sin on Your Dating Life

Chapter 9: Setting Smart Boundaries and Realistic Goals with the Opposite Sex

Chapter 11: "But I've Already Blown It—What Now?"

♥♥♥ ***58–139: Average to "ni-i-ice!" Get some "wait training" before you start.***

You're not alone—a lot of teens land in this dating, relating, waiting range. But with a little work, you can improve your DQ. We suggest you pay close attention to these chapters:

Chapter 4: Mixed Signals: Guy/Girl Communication
Differences
Chapter 5: Find a *Real* Person. . .Not a Hollywood
Myth
Chapter 10: Guilt-Free Sex, God's Way"

♥♥♥♥♥ *140–162: Absolute dating genius.*
You're headed in the right direction.

Congratulations! Your high DQ shows that you handle guy-girl relationships with maturity and that you're
committed to sexual purity. Now's the time to risk-proof
your future marriage by doing all you can to become the
kind of person your partner needs. We suggest you spend
a little extra time in these chapters:

Chapter 6: Seven Secrets Guys Need to Know about
Girls
Chapter 7: Seven Secrets Girls Need to Know about
Guys
Chapter 10: Guilt-Free Sex, God's Way
Chapter 12: Pray *Now* for Your Future Mate

CHAPTER 2

Getting Ready for the Dating-Relating Thing

Christ–Centered Strategies for Purity. . .
Plus Twelve Great Dates (and Five You'll Hate)

Here they are—three powerful ways to avoid sexual temptation and to pursue purity:

1. Set your standards now, and stick to them.
2. Draw a line that you will not cross. Define those areas you think are restricted to marriage. Consider those areas off-limits.
3. Don't test your limits. Don't play games with sexuality. Don't experiment to find out how far you can go without sinning.

Memorize these strategies, and choose to live by them *before* you start dating.

Committing yourself to purity doesn't happen by accident; it requires hard work and obedience to God. "Flee the evil desires of youth and pursue righteousness, faith, love and peace, along with those who call on the Lord out of a pure heart" (2 Timothy 2:22 NIV).

It involves a very personal conviction that you aren't afraid to share in public.

Several years back, I (Michael) called a pack of teens from my church (guys who were in a discipleship group I led), then headed to a remote spot in the Rocky Mountains.

When my church group and I arrived at our destination, I shared a true story: "Let me tell you about a man who lost his life to AIDS a few years back. This guy had his ashes sprinkled right here. Before his death, he committed his heart to Jesus. But he also expressed some deep regrets for not being self-controlled as the Bible instructs. If he were alive today, he'd warn you not to follow the path he chose.

"Guys, you have a chance to honor God with your lives. Let's make a pact with God to live a life of purity."

Before returning home, each one of us slipped on cross necklaces and made vows to remain pure. Then we spent time sharing our struggles, reading scripture, and praying for one another.

I'm thrilled to report that years later the guys are still wearing their crosses—and are committed to saving themselves for their future brides.

Making a pact for purity is the place to start. (For some clues, take a look at our suggestions at the end of this chapter.) Your goal should be to surrender your sexuality to God so that He can sanctify it, bless it, and help you make it exactly what He designed it to be. This involves taking to heart the three strategies we mentioned above.

Let's zero in on each one.

STRATEGY 1: Set Your Standards

It's easy to feel confused about sex these days. Just look around: we live in a world that ignores or distorts what God says is good, and that all too often contradicts what He tells us is sinful. Even many Christians have differing viewpoints about human sexuality. But why go anyplace but the Source for answers? Why not trust the One who created sex?

The "Word of God"—the Holy Bible—is filled with the guidelines we need. And it's exactly the place to turn as we set standards for healthy dating and relating. Below are ten biblical values that can help you define your beliefs, attitudes, and choices about sexuality. Look up each scripture reference, and then apply the truth to your life.

Key Biblical Values

- *Job 31:1*—Make a covenant with your eyes to (1) keep your mind pure and (2) to resist looking lustfully at the opposite sex.
- *Psalm 119:9*—Commit to filling your mind and heart with God's Word, which can empower you to pursue purity.
- *John 10:10*—Use your freedom through Christ to become more like Him.
- *Romans 13:13–14*—Avoid sexual immorality, and learn to treat others with decency and respect.
- *1 Corinthians 6:18*—Avoid situations that may cause you to compromise your standards.
- *1 Corinthians 6:19–20*—Understand that your body is God's temple; refuse to defile it in any possible way.
- *2 Corinthians 10:5*—Strive to take every thought captive and make it obedient to Christ.
- *Philippians 2:4–7*—Become selfless, just as Christ is selfless; strive to care about the well-being of others, not just your own.
- *Philippians 4:8*—Fix your eyes on what is honorable and right, and set your mind on all that is pure, lovely, and admirable.
- *2 Timothy 2:22*—Run to God as fast as you can whenever you are tempted.

Ask Yourself Some Tough Questions
1. *Is purity really important to me?*
2. *How committed am I to saving myself for marriage?*
3. *Do I respect my dates, or am I causing them to compromise?*
4. *Will I be able to take a stand for purity even if my friends don't stand with me?*

Work It Out
In the space provided, jot down three scripture references (from the list above), along with a simple action plan—how I plan to live by these biblical standards:

_____

_____

_____

_____

_____

STRATEGY 2: Draw a Line. . .but Make It a Lifestyle
We hear it from guys and girls all the time: "How far is too far? What, specifically, does the Bible say I *can* and *can't* do?" In reality, some of us just want to know the "rules" so we can inch right up to the lines. But the problem is, we go crazy trying not to cross them. And an even bigger problem is, sometimes we do. So before you build a giant "sexual behavior boundary," choose to make purity your

lifestyle, not just another rule to follow. This involves a serious attitude adjustment. Remind yourself of these truths:

- *I choose a lifestyle of purity in order to be more like Christ (Ephesians 5:1–7).*
- *I choose a lifestyle of purity because this is how the Lord has called me to live (1 Thessalonians 4:3–8).*
- *I choose a lifestyle of purity because I want to spend eternity with God (Matthew 5:8).*

A teen who asked to remain anonymous told us this about choosing purity: "The way we can be pure is not by seeing how close we can get to the line without crossing it, but instead by seeing how close we can get to God. Each morning, I strive to make Hebrews 12:1–2 my prayer: 'Lord, help me to throw off the different sins that entangle me and allow me to run toward You with patient endurance.'"

With your attitude adjusted and your commitment set, it's time to draw the line.

First, understand the twelve steps of sexual intimacy: (1) eye-to-body—that first glance; (2) eye-to-eye—noticing each other; (3) voice-to-voice—talking to each other; (4) holding hands—the first touch; (5) arm-to-shoulder—you're a couple; (6) arm-to-waist—the relationship is getting serious; (7) short kisses on the cheek or lips—the focus is on each other; (8) intimate, extended-time kissing—sexual arousal is triggered; (9) hand-to-body—exploring each other's uniqueness while fully clothed or partially un-clothed; (10) being naked together—moving into the intimacy of Genesis 2:25; (11) hand-to-genital—exploring the "source of life" and ultimate pleasure; (12) genital-to-genital—the two become one through sexual intercourse.

Second, predetermine where you will stop. Making this decision ahead of time will help you when you're in the heat of the moment. Many teens draw the line somewhere between no. 4 and no. 7. Moving into no. 8 is a big mistake. And if you do, it should set off a loud mental alarm for you. Steps 8 and beyond are reserved for the wonderful, holy bonds of marriage between a man and a woman.

Third, talk openly about your commitment to purity. Early on in your dating relationship, tell your partner something like this: "I've made a commitment to purity, which means I care too much about you and both of our futures to let anything happen that we would regret. I think we should focus more on getting to know each other. . .and less on the physical." It's amazing how this step clears the air—and steers you away from a lot of heartache later. How? It minimizes the frustration and anger caused by false expectations. It also develops a kind of accountability. When the other person knows what the standards are, it's not quite so easy for the first one to forget them either. (You'll read more on this topic in chapter 9: "Setting Smart Boundaries and Realistic Goals with the Opposite Sex.")

Ask Yourself Some Tough Questions

1. *What are my limits physically with my date—hand holding, a short kiss?*
2. *What physical activities would cause me to slide down that slope to sexual activity?*
3. *How can I keep myself from inching too close to the line I've drawn?*
4. *What will I do if my date doesn't share my values?*

Work It Out

In the space provided, write a prayer to Jesus, asking Him to help you to live for Him and to pursue purity:

_____

_____

_____

_____

_____

STRATEGY 3: Don't Test Your Limits

God is less impressed with your ability to stand up to sin and more impressed by the obedience you show when you run from it. Take a look at what pastor and author Joshua Harris says on this issue:

Physical interaction encourages us to start something we're not supposed to finish, awakening desires we're not allowed to consummate, turning on passions we have to turn off. What foolishness! The Bible tells us the path of sin, particularly in regard to the wrong use of our sexuality, is like a highway to the grave. We shouldn't get on it, then try to stop before we arrive at the destination—God tells us to stay off that highway completely.[1]

So once you've set your standards, stick to them. Here's how:

1. *Be secure in your self-identity.* Know yourself and be your own person. If you're confident of your identity, you will be free to be yourself and to accept others as they are without conforming to their expectations or condoning their behavior.

2. *Know your weak areas.* The enemy will attack where you're most vulnerable, and the easiest targets are the eyes

and ears. Kevin, a high school junior, openly admits he used to be the one who told the dirty jokes along with friends and even became addicted to pornography in junior high. Hanging out with certain people and watching certain TV shows constantly fed his addiction. "Anytime I was tempted, I'd pray. I just realized that the more I focused on God, [the struggle] wasn't so hard anymore."

3. *Find accountability.* Find a trustworthy adult leader, gather some friends, and start a group at your church or school. The first thing you should hold each other accountable for is your walk with God. Have a devotional time three times each week, consisting of worship, Bible reading, and prayer time. Here's your goal: spend a lot of time with God in His Word, replacing lust with a love for God. The second area of accountability is sexual temptation. Read a book on purity—hmmm, we have a pretty good suggestion (like maybe the one you're holding)! A book like this can help your group to talk openly about sexual issues. But prepare yourself: the discussion can feel a bit shocking and a little embarrassing at times, but it's a great way to help each other *live* your commitment to purity.

Ask Yourself Some Tough Questions
1. *How do I see myself?*
2. *Am I a person whose actions are determined by my personal set of values?*

3. *Do I act the way I do to gain the acceptance and approval of others?*

4. *Who's calling the shots in my life—me or my friends?*

Work It Out

In the space provided, jot down three ways you will resist testing your limits: _____

_____

_____

_____

_____

Make a Pact for Purity with Your Family

Next to committing your life to Christ, this is one of the most important decisions you'll make as a young man or young lady. And even if you have already done something like this at youth group, it's more powerful if you have this experience with Mom and Dad. (So definitely share this page with your parents.)

Here's how a "Family Pact for Purity" works:

1. Set aside uninterrupted time and find a private place. Acquire a cross necklace, a ring, or a watch beforehand and have your parents present it to you as a symbol of purity.

2. Read 2 Timothy 2:14–26. Go back and reread verse

15. Tell what it means to you to be "one approved." Now reread verse 22. Tell how you will "live" these verses. (Hint: accountability from your family, your friends, and your church.)

3. Tell why you're making this commitment. For example, "I'm saving myself for my future husband because. . ." or "I desire to be a godly man and pursue purity because. . ."

4. Spend some time praying with your parents.

• Ask God for strength and guidance.

• Ask God to help you treat your date the same way you want someone to treat the person you will someday marry.

• Ask God to help you behave on dates in such a way that you would never be afraid of your future spouse meeting any of your former dates.

Twelve Great Dates (and Five You'll Hate)

Dating shouldn't trigger more fear than a trip to the dentist's office. If you're going to date, get off the emotional roller coaster! Keep in mind that at this stage, your focus should be on friendship not romance. This approach takes away a lot of pressure and keeps your times together enjoyable. Most of all, it allows you to get to know each other. We've filled these paragraphs with creative dating ideas that will help you maximize the fun.

Dates under $20

Enjoy a kid's meal (big-kid style). Whether or not you grew up eating in fast-food restaurants, this experience will take you back to your childhood. The meals are relatively small, but the toys have come a long way.

Ride a bus—anywhere. This date offers a chance to be spontaneous while exploring the world of mass transit. Grab a map and let someone else do the driving. (Don't forget your cell phone so you can check in with Mom and Dad.)

Play a mean round of Putt-Putt. It's amazingly fun to knock around brightly colored golf balls on artificial grass. Test your skill as you navigate windmills, streams, elephants, and any other obstacle that stands in your way.

Have some major fun at a minor-league game. Baseball can be exciting at any level. But it's great to watch minor-league players battle for a spot in the majors. And the roasted peanuts are a must.

Adventure Dates

Take on a megacoaster. Loop, lunge, plunge, zip, flip, whirl. If your stomach can hold up, it's an awesome feeling having your mind rattled and your body flung in a zillion different directions. Today's megacoasters are faster, higher, and wilder—not to mention safer—and use the latest computer technology. Some cars run backward, some are suspended below the track, and others blast through dark tunnels with special effects, such as laser shows, smoke, and music.

Become fat-tire fanatics (try mountain biking). While mountain biking is one of those grab-some-wheels-and-just-do-it sports, my (Michael's) inaugural blaze down a trail with my date (who is now my wife) taught me a valuable lesson: (Inexperience + Pride + Pedals) x Tricky Mountain Trails = DISASTER. But you'll have a great time if you follow two rules of the road: (1) Never tackle more trail than you can handle; (2) Don't be kamikazes—defined by those in the sport as "idiots who scream down trails, endangering the physical and mental safety of others."

Learn to snowboard. If you can resist feeling self-conscience around your date—and count your first day on the slopes as the toughest—the two of you will have a good time mastering this sport together. Snowboarding has a really fast learning curve, especially compared to skiing and surfing.

Dates While You Wait

Make a date with Barnes & Noble. Spend a couple hours at Barnes & Noble, Mardel, Family Christian Stores (or one of your other favorite book outlets), and pick out devotional guides for each other. Then linger over a cup of tea or coffee, reading a devotional entry, as well as sharing why you picked this particular book for your date.

Get grungy for God. If your church hosts a workday, consider volunteering for an afternoon of loving sacrifice. This faith-focused date may involve some humble service: painting the sanctuary, scrubbing floors, cleaning nursery toys. But as you roll up your sleeves and break a sweat with your date, the two of you will have fun serving your church and discovering the depth of each other's heart for God.

Host a Super Bowl party. All you need are sodas, snacks, a TV (preferably big-screen with surround sound), and a bunch of sports-crazed friends. Plan this party with your partner—make it a date! This really is a great idea for new couples. Because it's a group setting, you don't have to worry about the awkwardness of a one-on-one date. Most of all, the two of you will share some laughs as you root for your favorite team.

Distribute some next-to-new care packages. Most of us accumulate more stuff than we need. It's fulfilling to give away some of it instead of just piling it in a long-forgotten corner of our closet. Here's an idea that lets you and your date bless the life of another with something you no longer need.

Dates You'll Hate

If you're heading off on a first date, absolutely do *not*...

Swim together. It's just a good idea to avoid any situation that requires bathing suits. There is no need to make yourself any more self-conscious as you try to make a good first impression.

Eat spaghetti. Italian restaurants are great for ambiance as long as you don't try to eat spaghetti in front of your date. There is too much of a risk for slurping or dropping tomato sauce down the front of your shirt.

Go to an "ex-date hangout." Never make this type of comment on a first date: "Yeah, Eric and I used to come here every Friday night," or "Britney always loved this restaurant's chocolate malts."

Watch a flesh-filled flick. Carefully choose a movie. At least check out the ratings so you are not bombarded with sex and nudity. It can be very embarrassing as you sit next to someone you are trying desperately to impress.

Go on a "speedy date." Make sure you plan wisely. Dates might not feel very special if they have to be scheduled between favorite TV shows and time with friends.

Consider a Non-dating Alternative

What on earth are we talking about? First, let's define these two terms. Dating is usually one-on-one and is accompanied by such things as a romantic atmosphere, sweaty palms, a lump in the throat, and the desire to sound intelligent. A non-date, on the other hand, usually takes place in a group setting—less formal, no romantic atmosphere, and most of all, less pressure. In other words, you have a better chance to be *yourself*.

The point is, unless you're a born conversationalist, sometimes it's easier to get to know someone in a less-pressured, non-date situation. It's also easier to ask someone out on a non-date. Here's an example:

> *Date:* "Hey, Sara, would you. . .uh. . .I mean. . .uh. . .how about you and me. . .uh. . ."

Pretty smooth, eh? But a non-date is easier.

> *Non-date:* "Hey, Sara, a bunch of us are getting together for some volleyball at the park this Saturday. Want to come?"

If she turns you down, it's no big deal, because you weren't asking her out on a *date* anyway. And you can walk away with your self-esteem intact.[2]

CHAPTER 3

Finding and Attracting
the *Right* Person

---

*What to Say, What to Wear,
and How to Put Your Best Face Forward*

It was well before I (Michael) had gotten married. I was fresh out of college, single. . .and I'd finally landed a date with Eilene—a young lady I really wanted to impress. To me, she had the right qualities: she shared so many of my interests in music and art and politics, she was fun and down-to-earth, and she loved the outdoors.

"*Yes!*" I screamed as I hung up my phone and broke into a "victory" dance. We had decided to go horseback riding at her uncle's ranch. "She likes me! Next Saturday it's off to the mountains with Eilene!"

I didn't think anything could possibly go wrong. I imagined riding side by side through a peaceful valley filled with little creatures like Bambi and Thumper.

It'll be romantic, I thought. *I'll gently take her hand, and we'll ride into the sunset together.*

But there was one tiny little detail I overlooked: I had never been on a horse in my life. I had ridden a donkey at an amusement park once when I was ten—but never a horse on steep trails in the hills.

No problem, I thought. *I've seen lots of John Wayne movies. I'll just imitate the Duke. She'll think I was born on a stallion!*

That Saturday, after being chased by a pack of scrubby-looking dogs and nearly thrown off Chester, my spooked horse, I suddenly realized I had a serious problem. Here I was, screaming at the top of my lungs, bouncing like a yo-yo on a string as I clung to the back of this frightened beast. And it seemed like old Chester—who was prime glue-factory material—reached unheard of speeds as he galloped down hills, through dry riverbeds, and under low-hanging branches.

"Michael! Are you okay? You could have been killed!" Eilene yelled when she caught up to us. She began to calm Chester. I slithered off the horse and hugged the ground for a while.

"Huh? Yeah, I'm fine. How about if we just walk the horses through that safe meadow then head back to your uncle's place," I suggested.

Big mistake.

By this time, I was an emotional mess. I couldn't talk or walk—at least like a human. I resembled a bowlegged chimp, and I sounded like one, too. Sadly enough, my dating nightmare didn't end here.

As we made our way through a field, a long, green grasshopper decided to wander across my shoes, up one of my legs, and into my pants. I didn't detect the little guy until he reached my back pocket. Then I let out a blood-curdling yell and began to swat wildly at my jeans.

Eilene looked on in horror. She never went out with me again.

Are We Trying Too Hard?

Dating blunders. Trying too hard to live up to an expectation that no human can attain. Crashing conversations. First impressions that seem to bomb. Sound familiar?

It all spells the same thing: I-N-S-E-C-U-R-I-T-Y.

But whether we like it or not, ours is a society of packaging. Sadly, first impressions count. Even if you're the coolest, most amazing person on the face of the planet—which you are! Even if you really deserve a chance with your date, you probably won't get past the first one if insecurity gets in the way.

Let's focus our attention on a tip some people already know: you have to "package" yourself if you're even going to have a chance.

We know what you're thinking: *Why should Christians have to do that? Shouldn't people just accept us the way we are? "Packaging" sounds like deception.*

Actually, it's not. What we're talking about is liking the person you are on the *inside* and then learning to put your best foot forward. That's just plain smart, not to mention practical. The first impression you make comes from your appearance—both external *and* internal. A friend once said, "It's not merely the way you style your hair. Your appearance also involves body language, facial expressions (smiles or frowns), the position of your body, how you walk. . .and confidence that comes from the inside. It's a self-transformation strategy."

So what's the best way to work through the dating jitters, put your best foot forward, and achieve a happy dating, relating future?

It all begins as you strive to be the best person you can be! Love your life and make it into the adventure it was meant to be, even if your life is hard or difficult. In other words, attitude is everything. We all live in our very own Lord of the Rings story with ups, downs, challenges, and victories. But just like Frodo's story, you need to have a plan. You need to surround yourself with people you can trust, people who will walk with you no matter what.

(Remember what happened in *The Fellowship of the Ring*?) And maybe someday you will have your own "ring" of power and love—but avoid the ones with Elven writing on the inside!

What other steps should you take? Try this eight-point plan. It won't eliminate every dating blunder, but it's a practical way to polish your package. And that will boost your self-confidence.

1. Stop Looking for Love in All the Wrong Places

Can you make a list of all the wrong places to look for a godly mate? Go ahead! We bet you can list at least three off the top of your head.

If you're looking for someone who will love you madly, purely, and faithfully, you will find them in places you love to be, doing things you love to do. . .just being "you." One of the most important things about finding a godly mate is to *be* a godly mate.

As you become the best "you" you can be with God's help, it will help if you become involved in activities and groups that are most likely to be attended by the kind of man or woman you would like to meet. Think outside the box! Join a club, volunteer, try something new, and find ways to meet new people.

Sometimes new friends will open doors to new

experiences. The goal is to reach out and explore while remembering the core of who you are.

The most important "appearance" a person can present has little to do with how they look. Someone who is attracted to you may initially see your outward appearance as attractive or not. But it's your friendship, spirit, and personality, your integrity and trustworthiness that will keep them coming back for more. And those are the foundational attributes of a godly mate on which to build a really terrific long-lasting relationship.

Before we get into the outward tools of attracting a date, let's talk about our "inward apparel" and how to put on the beauty and strength that God has created inside us.

2. Learn to Like the Person God Created You to Be

It's no secret that our society is hung up on outward appearances and the aura of success. If you don't look like a celebrity on a magazine cover or one of the many reality stars on TV, you don't measure up by popular standards.

But in God's kingdom, we are all royalty. If you are a son or daughter of Jesus, then you are heirs of His kingdom. We all get to be Prince William and Princess Kate! God measures beauty and strength from within, and that's how we should measure ourselves—and others!

Comparing yourself to the superficial standards of the

culture around you is a recipe for disaster. Just like a train headed down the track at crazy speeds without brakes, when it hits a curve, it's going to go off the rails! You can see many examples of rich and famous beautiful people "going off the rails" because they have no self-control, no "brakes" to stop them.

That's what our culture is training us to do. Without putting on the brakes and slowing down and really seeing the danger in those superficial values, the lives of millions of teenagers and young adults—many of them are your friends—are going to run off the tracks and wreck their lives because their self-confidence is weak. And that's a difficult thing to deal with.

3. Don't Be Plastic

When I (Tess) was in college, a godly young woman named Peggy stood up in chapel one morning to pray. And what she said blew me away. It rocked my world and sent me reeling. Very simply, she said, "God, please take all the plastic out of me and make me real and teach me how to love you."

Plastic. How much of you is plastic?

We become plastic when we create a persona of outward appearances and behavior that make us more attractive to others while covering up our true identity.

We become more and more plastic as we seek to live our lives for the acceptance of those around us and push away the real "us" that we were created to be. Before long, you may find yourself rejecting others who don't fit into you little circle of friends that you call your "world."

Pinocchio was the name of a wooden puppet that wanted to be a real boy. But he had a habit of lying (which is another way of not being real). Every time he told a lie, his nose would grow longer. It took him further away from being a real boy. But when he finally learned to love the truth and stop lying the magic of that re-created him into a real human boy and he became a son to Giuseppe, his maker.

When we choose to be puppets of the society around us, caring about what our friends think of us more than we care about what God says about us, or we conform to friends' expectation out of fear of rejection, we often lie about who we really are in order to be accepted. In Pinocchio's life, that meant he stayed wooden. For us, it's plastic.

In the world of dating and relating, girls and guys do this all the time to put on a good front for the person they want a relationship with. They can maintain this kind of phony exterior self for a long, long time. Sometimes it's not until well into the relationship or even after marriage that some people discover the true identity of their partner.

Not a good kind of surprise at all.

That's why it's so important to really get to know the person before you begin to date them. See them in every season, in every kind of situation. What do they look like on the *inside*? How do they "wear" stress? Anger? Financial loss? How do they treat strangers? Do they blame others? Do they strike out? Do they put people down and take no responsibility? How is their prayer life? Do they lie, cheat, or steal? When you are interested in someone, open your eyes and take the time to *see* them for who they really are, not what you want them to be.

As we walk with Jesus, the Holy Spirit will reveal our identity to us and also give us insight and discernment into the identity of others and help us to stay *real*!

As Mahatma Gandhi said, "Be the change that you wish to see in the world." If you are willing to be different and use a godly standard to evaluate the lives of those you are attracted to, then finding a godly mate will become a lot easier.

4. Give Some Attention to Your Inward Clothing

Whether you're male or female, grace is a standard of living that transcends crudeness, anger, self-doubt, and fear. Grace treats others not according to what they deserve, but instead with kindness and understanding no matter how bad the behavior. We all need grace at some point in our lives, and we should all give grace when we can. With grace, you don't get what you deserve; you get love and mercy. And a grace-filled person is the type you should be searching for.

So go ahead and "put on" grace. It's the type of "clothing" that another person will see on you and will immediately find attractive. Grace is glue; it helps bind people together. Grace is the positive to the negative others often exude. Grace draws people in and gives them a safe place to be themselves.

What other "clothing" should we put on?

Let's consider self-control for a moment. Some people consider self-control to be a drag. I'm sure you know people who live by the motto "Just let me do what I want! Nobody's getting hurt!"

What a cop-out! Every action we initiate has ripple effects that we cannot control. So we need to control ourselves. Doing the right thing, living with grace toward others, and being trustworthy should be our norm. Grace and self-control are *very* attractive.

What else will a potential godly mate be looking for? Mercy. If you are constantly comparing them to others or expecting them to always do the right thing, then no one will ever be able to meet your expectations. And you'll end up making them feel frustrated and unworthy.

Mercy and forgiveness are an important "cloak" you can offer to others for their covering and protection from ridicule and humiliation. This makes you a safe person to be around. We all fall down. But it's the hand that forgives and lifts you up that you learn to trust. Mercy saves us. Mercy is attractive!

And finally, a very important piece of inward "apparel" is your own relationship with Jesus. Here are some questions you can ask yourself about your own heart (and the heart of someone you're dating):

• Are you faking your Christianity?

• Do you have a genuine love relationship with the Son of God?

• What is your story? How did you come to faith in Jesus, and what have been the hallmarks of your walk with Him?

• In what ways is He re-creating you from the inside out?

• In what ways have you changed since you began walking your journey with Jesus?

• What has He said to you, and how did He say it? What have you learned?

• Do you listen to the guidance of the Holy Spirit as He leads you to make good decisions and choices?

• Do you allow Him full access to your heart, your mind, your spirit, and your life?

5. Focus on Your Faith

Stop for a minute and examine your life. Think about everything, both the good and the bad. Don't leave out the pain and the tough times. The old saying "What doesn't kill us makes us stronger" is so true. Even the scriptures say that Jesus "learned. . .from what he suffered" (Hebrews 5:8 NIV). And this was referring to his childhood!

Be willing to share your own hurts and failures with God and ask Him for grace, forgiveness, and mercy. And then share those things with someone you care about. Wisdom is attractive.

No matter how young or old you are, you have a story. What role has Christ played in your story? If his role has been weak, then that is something you can work on by allowing the Holy Spirit to transform your heart and spirit. This will deepen your walk with God and strengthen your foundation of faith.

Being a Christian isn't about which church you attend or doing all the "dos" and not doing any of the "don'ts." It's about developing a deep love relationship with Jesus. And through this process, the Holy Spirit teaches us who we were created to be.

6. Consider Your Outward Clothing

How many of us are style challenged? For the longest time as a young woman I was completely clueless about style. No matter how much I liked a current style of clothing, when I went shopping it always seemed that I came home with the same baggy, oversized tops and stretch pants in the same dark colors. There was just so much fear in trying something new, and I had such a bad body image that I just wanted to cover everything up and not think about how I wasn't as beautiful as some of the girls I admired in college. So what happened?

I began to think about what I wore. One day my dear friend Rhea, who was so beautiful and talented, asked me why I never wore any colors. She complimented me and told me she thought I had a cute figure but couldn't understand why I was hiding it. She worked at the Estee Lauder counter at my favorite department store and offered to go shopping with me one day to help me buy some new clothes with her store discount.

The day arrived, and when I got to the store, she had already picked out some beautiful clothes in my size that I would never have chosen for myself. As I tried on each outfit, her encouraging remarks (and the cute girl I saw for the first time in the mirror) convinced me that I could be something more than I ever thought I could be! I walked out of the store with a whole new wardrobe, but more importantly, a whole new attitude about myself and how I looked.

Whether you're a young man or young woman, you can change yourself. You can allow the clothes you choose to say something about who you feel you are, how you feel about yourself, and the kind of attitude you have about life. It doesn't have to have anything to do with what people expect you to be, but rather should be a reflection of your vision for your life and the real you.

There are lots of great resources online to help you pick clothes that match your build or figure. Pay attention to some of those tips to help you choose clothing that will accentuate your natural strength or beauty. There are even sites to help you discover the best tones and colors to match your skin.

Again, this is all about you feeling and appearing like *you*, not some supermodel or celebrity. Your own natural strength and beauty are what attract someone to you. Your clothes simply help to tell your story without you ever opening your mouth (except to smile!).

I learned the importance of healthy eating. It goes without saying that your body is the temple of the Holy Spirit. When you become a son or daughter of God, the Spirit dwells in your spirit and you become His dwelling place.

So keeping your body healthy and strong is important. Eating healthy foods helps keep your skin looking good, keeps your weight under control, and provides the fuel your body needs to be adventurous and stay active with your friends or participate in any sports you might enjoy.

That doesn't mean you can't enjoy those BBQ wings without licking your fingers or take a big bite of your favorite slice of pizza! But it does mean that if you respect your own body, your future mate will, too! People notice those things.

Stay clean, be active, get enough sleep, brush your teeth, wash your hair, wear clean clothes, cut your nails, and remember to smile. When you smile, look someone full in the face, make eye contact, and make your smile genuinely say, "Hello!" Even across a crowded room, a great smile can be the most intimate form of communication. Be assured that a great smile draws people to you and makes them want to know you. So does being able to laugh at yourself and having a good sense of humor, especially when things are tough or not going your way.

Okay, So Let's Recap. . .

Putting your best "face" forward involves being healthy, taking care of yourself, being *you* and not a plastic copy of everyone else, dressing neatly and cleanly and appropriately for the occasion, having a great smile and good sense of humor, and having something to start or continue a conversation. In all this, your inward "apparel" is more important than your outward appearance in the long run. Put on grace, mercy, kindness, and self-control, and be humble.

Putting on these attributes of Christ is the best foundation for a happy relationship. You don't just wake up one day and—*bam!*—you're a great partner. You have to start working on "you" now. Every little decision you make from today forward creates that person you want to become. Surrender to Jesus every day and seek His heart, and He will create that man or woman in you.

Finally, remember the fruits of allowing the Spirit to guide and change you: "What happens when we live God's way? He brings gifts into our lives, much the same way that fruit appears in an orchard—things like affection for others, exuberance about life, serenity. . . . Among those who belong to Christ, everything connected with getting our own way and mindlessly responding to what everyone else calls necessities is killed off for good—crucified" (Galatians 5:22–23 MSG).

Get rid of the plastic. Be real.

CHAPTER 4

Mixed Signals:
Guy/Girl Communication Differences

How to Tune In and Connect

All evening Jordan had troubles talking to Kristen. Now he'd reached his breaking point. *What's with her? What does she want from me?*

It was a special night—Kristen's seventeenth birthday. Jordan had planned the perfect night: a movie, dinner at the nicest restaurant in town. . .lots of conversation.

The place where they had come to dine was filled with the usual buzz of couples talking, clinking silverware, and mouthwatering aromas. But Jordan and Kristen sat at opposite ends of the table, Kristen toying with her chicken salad and Jordan munching his barbecued ribs as he replayed the evening in his mind.

I picked her up at her house and whisked her off to what I was sure would be a knockout evening. In the car, I told her all about my day at school, and she—well, she didn't say a word.

Then, when I opened the door to the restaurant and commented about how I love coming here with her, that's when she lobbed a stinging comment: "Are you sure you mean me, or one of your past girlfriends?"

Jordan took a sip of water then cleared his throat. *Got to diffuse this bomb.* "Uh, look—out the window. Isn't that the most beautiful night sky you've ever seen?"

"It's okay. But I saw lightning. It'll rain soon. It always does."

Okay, new approach. "Uh, are you having a bad day or something?"

Kristen just glared at him.

Jordan leaned back in his chair. "Please, talk to me. What's wrong? Why are you acting this way on your special night—your birthday?"

That's when she let him have it. "A few days ago, you called me. 'Hello, Kristen,' you said. 'Let's do something perfect for your birthday. I have some ideas.'"

"'Perfect,'" I responded. " 'Can't wait!'"

"'Great,'" you said. " 'I'll work out the details, and then I'll call you.'"

"I was thrilled, but you never called back. . .until, let's see, two hours ago. Then you said you'd pick me up around six and didn't show up until almost seven. And so I just sat there, feeling very foolish, wondering if you would even come at all. Then my mind began to play games with me: *What if he got in an accident? Is he okay? Maybe he isn't interested in me anymore. Maybe he forgot about my birthday. Does he think the world revolves around him. . .and that I'm supposed to just wait here by the phone? What an insensitive jerk!"*

Kirsten moved forward and locked eyes with Jordan. "If you really care about me, then show some respect. Most of all. . .communicate with me!"

Jordan just sat at the table with his mouth wide open—and, as usual, he was unsure about what to say.

Basic Guy/Girl Connection Needs

Communication is the key to any relationship. If two people don't connect very well, or if one person in the relationship feels hurt or unheard, problems arise, individuals grow apart. . .and the connection disintegrates. It's not rocket science, right?

As you grow into adulthood and eventually marry (if that's God's will for you), you'll discover that the people you want to be closest to are—ironically—the ones who are sometimes deaf to the sound of your voice.

"I just can't read her sometimes!" husbands sometimes complain about their wives. "What did I do wrong?"

"Why won't he listen to me?" wives fire back. "It's like

he just doesn't hear me."

Sound familiar? Have you heard your parents say these things? (Have *you* ever felt this way about the opposite sex?) Most of us have experienced the emptiness that comes from feeling tuned out. That's because listening is an act of love—or, at a more basic level, an act of simple consideration.

All communication requires two basic things: a speaking voice and a listening ear. This sounds pretty simple, but it's not. Most of us are very selective listeners, tuning in and tuning out as our interests dictate. With all the extraneous noise and worthless static that bombards us daily, this skill can be a blessing. It is something else, however, when we find ourselves tuning out those we say we love.

Yet this is exactly how Kirsten felt: tuned out. And it hurt deeply because it came from the guy she was trying to connect with.

Through the months, Kirsten had invested her heart in this relationship—grounding it in friendship, faith, and purity. Though Jordan was a godly teen, it was important for the two of them to work through some communication "static." Getting to know each other better and having a healthy dating life depended on it. But most important of all, learning basic guy/girl communication skills as teenagers will help them as adults, enhancing future relationships—even strengthening their married lives.

A few days after expressing her frustration, Kirsten took one more step—writing a note that detailed her deepest "connection needs." What Kirsten shared applies to every couple:

Jordan, I need you to. . .
- *choke back the temptation to supply all the answers.*
- *take me seriously.*
- *not be uncomfortable with moments of silence.*
- *listen for more than just words. Listen to the feelings behind the words.*
- *affirm me for who I am and for who I am becoming.*
- *take my side at times.*
- *listen to me—with your ears and your heart.*

What Dating Couples Should Know. . .and *Do*

Get a clue about male/female communication differences. For guys, a conversation is often a way to define a problem, debate the rights and wrongs, and find a solution. But most females would rather have a friendly ear from a guy instead of advice. Teen girls often view a conversation as a way of sharing their emotions with the listener. They talk until they feel better. Guys, on the other hand, sometimes run out of words and shut down. (They simply don't know what else to talk about.) Understanding communication styles and differences will enable you to connect better with the opposite sex.

Make sure your date has been heard. Next to being a good listener, guys and girls both need to be understood. So don't just nod your head a few times and think you're doing your date a favor. Hear the other person's heart. Engage in the conversation and show that you really care what your date is thinking and feeling.

Connect with encouraging words. Mark Twain once said he could go for two months on a good compliment. Likewise, every one of us needs to be appreciated—to be applauded—for the awesome and unique person God made us. We need others to recognize our strengths or sometimes just to prop us up in the places where we tend to lean a little. Honest compliments are simple and cost nothing to give, but we must not underestimate their worth. Ladies, follow Kirsten's lead: consider sharing this need with your date. And guys, get a clue!

Be sensitive about your date's looks. That kind of joke hurts to the core—for both guys and girls. Make enough of them and you may condemn yourself to a life of being dateless. Moreover, the choice of joke material says more about the joker than it does about the joke's victim. Humor tends to reflect the fixations of a person's mind. If all you can joke about are body parts, you had better ask yourself where your thoughts are traveling.

Leave the crude jokes back in middle school. It's time to grow up a bit. References to bodily functions, noises, and smells reveal serious immaturity. Likewise, sex can be discussed openly, in a way that honors God, in a way that pushes the two of you to greater purity. (We trust this book is a good example of that.) But bedroom humor can be downright trashy and dishonoring to each other—and to God.

For guys only: Forget bragging; ask girls questions about their lives. A guy who can't help talking about himself around girls is a self-serving jerk. He's merely out to impress, and his core motive is to use. Any girl who falls for such a guy is a flake. Inevitably, she'll come out of the relationship disillusioned, empty, and wondering why this guy never cared about her as much as she did him. A true gentleman impresses girls by accident, through a genuine interest in their lives. And that sincerity will carry itself into a healthy marriage relationship.

For girls only: Keep confidences under verbal lock and key. If a guy confides in you and finds out the next day that he was yesterday's lunchroom dialogue, you deserve to be dumped. He's trusted you with something near and dear. Respect knows how to keep that trust.[1]

Good Conversation Is Key

Being a good conversationalist can be tricky at first. It may take a little practice before you become comfortable creating a conversation out of thin air. But we can't emphasize enough how important it is. When you look someone in the eye and ask good questions, it makes them feel that you are truly interested in them as a person. This works with girls, boys, kids, adults, employers, little old ladies, check-out clerks at the store, and even your own parents. It's an art form that you develop over time.

One really good way to make a great impression conversationally is to ask questions! The typical "What do you like to do?" "What classes are you taking?" "What did you think about that test?" or "How 'bout them Lakers [or pick your sports team]?" is never a bad place to start. Ask about hobbies, travels, family, or favorite movies, etc. Or talk about something *you* like and see if they catch interest. (Take a look at our suggestions below.)

For Christians it's important to be able to discuss your faith and your beliefs, talk about your relationship with God and your journey. Be honest and be humble about your walk with God. People like to know you're human, just like them. Being interested in someone else's life, learning their interests and what gives them joy, as well as sharing in their hurts and challenges is a very godly trait—and it's very attractive!

Eight Great Conversation Starters

In case you need a jump start, get your date talking with these conversation starters:

After-school jobs. This will reveal a lot about your date—and it gives you lots of ground to cover. "It's so cool that you work at a veterinary clinic. Is that what you plan to study in college?" "What's it like making pizzas?" "Do you like working at your dad's store?"

Animals. People love to talk about their four-legged friends. "Do you have a pet?" "What's its name?" "How long have you had it?"

Embarrassing moments. We all love to laugh, especially at ourselves. Pull stories from the "I-Was-So-Embarrassed Files" of your life. You know—like the time you went horseback riding with someone you really, really wanted to impress and ended up getting a grasshopper caught in your pants! Oh wait. . .that was me (Michael). Never mind!

Faith. Here's a big part of your life you both have in common (assuming he or she is a Christian, which we hope is the case). Talk about what's going on in youth group, ministries you're involved in, great things God is doing in your life.

Hobbies. The sky's the limit here. Talk about sports, music, arts and crafts, unique excursions you've taken—anything!

Shopping. "Where'd you get that necklace? It looks very exotic!" Or "I'm looking for a new gaming system. Got any ideas?"

Vacations. There's so much to talk about—traveling, dream vacations, adventure trips. . .crazy places you've visited. Be Creative: "Let's say your parents offered to take you and a friend anywhere you want to go in the world next summer. What kind of vacation would you choose?"

You. As we mentioned earlier, be careful with this topic. If you talk too much about yourself, your date will think you're self-centered. Without bragging or sounding stuck on yourself (or spilling too many of your deepest, darkest secrets), fill your date in on what's unique about yourself—your hopes, dreams, goals, and interests.

Clear Up the Communication Static

Conversation #1—How It Could Be

Your Date: "I really hate this restaurant, and I don't see why you insist on coming here. What's a *runza* anyway, and why do you like them so much?"

You: "I hear you; I crave these things and you don't. But do you think you could order something else on the menu? And next time we can go to your favorite place."

Your Date: "Yeah, I guess so. I'll order a salad or

something. But when it's my turn to choose, we're heading to the sushi place across town!"

You: "Gross! I hate raw fish, but I'll do it. Thanks for coming here."

Your Date: "No problem. That's what couples do, right? They compromise."

Conversation #2—How It Usually Is

Your Date: "I really hate this restaurant, and I don't see why you insist on coming here. What's a *runza* anyway, and why do you like them so much?"

You: "You complain every time I even mention the word *runza*. What's your problem? Look—I like this food, so get over it!"

Your Date: "You never listen to me when I disagree with you about something. Why can't you see things my way? Why can't you stop being so selfish and think about me for a change?"

You: "Because it's always your way or the highway—and I'm tired of it."

Your Date: "I'm starting to get tired of these arguments. Why can't we connect?"

So which conversation is more common with your friends and family—even those you date? Let us guess—the

73

second one! Too bad, because Conversation 1 isn't that far out of touch with reality. In fact, with some work, it can actually be the regular mode of conversation. But it all begins with an important nine-letter word: *listening*.

"Guys just don't listen to me" is the anthem of many teen girls. Likewise, it's a complaint echoed by young men: "I can't get through to her—she just doesn't hear me."

Listening is where effective communication really begins. Instead of engaging in a verbal tug-of-war with people in your life, follow these essential steps:

Begin with passive listening (or silence). Give the other person a chance to speak their mind. "I'm just not getting anything out of band and really want to drop out. I can't keep up, and the teacher always embarrasses me in front of everyone."

Give acknowledgment responses. Don't just stand there with a blank expression on your face. Even when you're listening passively, it's a good idea to make sincere comments, such as "I see" or "Oh?" that emphasize that you are paying attention.

Offer a "door opener." This is a simple, nonjudgmental statement, such as, "How would you feel about talking to the teacher after class? Maybe she'll ease up on you." How-you-feel questions are less threatening to others, and they help spark communication.

Exercise active listening with a communication style called "shared meaning." Here's how it works:

1. You're frustrated because your date was late picking you up for dinner, and he didn't even bother to call you; he just showed up on your doorstep. So you approach him and say, "We need to talk about this. I'd like you to hear my side."

2. Once you have his attention, you explain your point of view (which you've thought through ahead of time) without being interrupted.

3. Next, your date repeats what he heard you say.

4. You then clarify or confirm what he said, ensuring that your thoughts and feelings have been heard accurately.

5. The process continues with him sharing his point of view and you listening and repeating what he said.

The goal of shared meaning is to be heard accurately. And once you've had a chance to state your case and listen to that of another person, the foundation is set for communication—and for a fair solution to the problem at hand. A solution that's grounded on listening and being heard. . .not just another pointless Tuesday night fight.

CHAPTER 5

Find a *Real* Person. . .
Not a Hollywood Myth

Leave Fantasyland:
The Real World of Love and Relationships

It's out there. . .everywhere you look. We are bombarded with the myth of the perfect boyfriend or girlfriend. But it's just a big fantasy, a Hollywood formula that rarely, if ever, actually happens. But it's been very successful for Hollywood as we continue to "buy it"—literally. We spend a lot of money on movies, TV shows, music, and books that play into our daydream of finding that one special person who will meet all of our needs. You know the dream— you lock eyes with someone across the room and then fall madly in love. There will be obstacles, but your love will overcome and you will live happily ever after. It makes for a good story. But it rarely happens in real life.

Have you been raised on a steady diet of this myth? Have you ever noticed all of the overt and subliminal messages from commercials and TV about how important it is to be beautiful, skinny or buff, rich and popular in order to be considered a human being "worth" being noticed or included? Have you believed the lie?

Nearly every TV show is about beautiful, rich people meeting and hooking up with other beautiful, rich people. . .or plain people trying to look beautiful and rich in order to be accepted in society and considered valuable. So unrealistic! It's not real. Don't buy into it. Remember, they get paid to make you wish you had their lives. If you stripped away their money and fame, you would be able to see that they are struggling with the same challenges that all of us normal people are dealing with. You are just taking yourself down a path of discontent and unhappiness if you chase after the fake lives of others. It will only lead to death of your spirit and your self-esteem. Stick to your true path and avoid comparing your journey to that of others. It's just a waste of time.

Let's Get Real

In real life, long-lasting relationships are built over time through experience and friendship, and by creating trust and respect. But that's not the story we often hear. It's tough to sort through what's real and what's fake. Peer pressure and bullying abound. Many of the violent episodes we hear about on the news occurred because someone was marginalized, rejected, bullied, and did not measure up to what the popular crowd determined was "normal" or "valuable."

Being devalued and humiliated, shamed or rejected is enough to make a lot of people become involved in violence, drugs, sex, alcohol, or even suicide. Girls and guys will compromise their faith and be unequally tied to people who don't share their faith or belief system just to conform and fit in and avoid ridicule and humiliation or bullying. The good news is God wants to help protect you and help you navigate through some of those difficult, dangerous waters. Just ask Him and He will (Psalm 140).

The Pursuit of "Wholeness"

Here is the truth and the good news of what God says:

- You are created uniquely, and God places great value on you (Psalm 139:14).
- You are dearly loved, and God is with you in Spirit all the time and walks with you in every situation (Psalm 139:1–12, 17–18). He is *for you!*
- Your glory and worth are determined by God and no one else (not even yourself—because we sometimes don't see or believe in our own worth) (Malachi 3:17; John 17:22).

- We are all "broken" in some way, but God desires to fill us with His love and Spirit and to heal us and make us "whole."

- You are never alone (Deuteronomy 31:6; Hebrews 13:5).

- You have been graced with unique gifts, talents, and desires. You have a destiny. You have a future and a hope that has nothing to do with how the world around you sees or values you (Jeremiah 29:11–13).

- The world will reject you just as it rejected Jesus, but He has overcome the world system, and through His love for you, you can persist and conquer and be victorious over the system (John 17).

- God has created His own system and His own kingdom, and as a part of Him, you will rule and reign in this spiritual kingdom here on earth as his son or daughter (Psalm 22:28; 103:19; Romans 14:16–19).

- God will give you power to realize who He has created you to be and will empower you to rise above everything that's thrown at you (2 Timothy 1:7, 2 Peter 1:3).

- Humans are not perfect, but God is, and He desires to share His perfection (or "wholeness") with us on an inward journey designed to make us great and good people (Philippians 2:14–16; Colossians 3:14; James 1:4; 1 John 4:12).

The Result of "Wholeness"

Many people will stay in a bad relationship because they feel incomplete if they are not a part of a "couple." It's like a section of them is missing if there isn't someone attached to their hand. They are holding on to the idea that that one person can fill those empty holes, heal them, and make them "whole."

Henri Nouwen, in his book *Reaching Out, Three Spiritual Movements*, from a chapter titled "A Suffocating Loneliness," says this:

There is much mental suffering in our world.
But some of it is suffering for the wrong reason
because it is born out of the *false expectation that
we are called to take each other's loneliness away.*

When our loneliness drives us away from
ourselves into the arms of our companions in life,
we are, in fact, driving ourselves into *excruciating
relationships, tiring friendships, and suffocating
embraces.*

To wait for moments or places where no pain
exists, no separation is felt and where all human
restlessness has turned into inner peace is waiting
for a dream world.

No friend or lover, no husband or wife, no

community or commune will be able to put to rest our deepest cravings for unity and wholeness.

And by burdening others with these divine expectations. . .we might inhibit the expression of free friendship and love and instead evoke feelings of inadequacy and weakness.

Friendship and love cannot develop in the form of an anxious clinging to each other. They ask for gentle fearless space in which we can move to and from each other.[1]

We should *not* be looking for someone to fix us, heal us, or make us whole. Only God can do that. And, as Nouwen said above, putting those "divine expectations" on someone else only sets us up for disappointment, hurt, and failed relationships. It makes us needy and weak. Wise up and stop trying to fix yourself by filling your life with more of the wrong solution.

What God Does

God desires to open up your heart and mind and show you the depths of who you are: your true identity, your talents, gifts, and also your weaknesses and vulnerabilities. As we journey inward, with Him as our guide, we discover more and more goodness about ourselves, more of the hidden treasures He has created inside us that need to be "mined" and brought into the light. We are His "jewels," and He is determined to cut and shape and polish us to "perfection."

The cutting and polishing can be painful. But the result is brilliance. This is the process that God undertakes when we invite Him to be our guide into the depths of our hearts. He cuts deep to reveal what's inside us: impurities that need to be cut out as well as the glory that needs to be revealed. Knowing our vulnerabilities and weaknesses will help us guard our hearts, for they determine the course of our lives (see Proverbs 4:23). Know that even in the midst of this remarkable process, God is guarding and guiding us all the way on the journey to wholeness.

Wholeness in Dating

When you consider going out with someone and having a real relationship with them, you must first have an idea of what kind of person you are looking for. But one thing is for sure: if you base your desire for a person on the myth of Hollywood perfection, you are setting yourself up for failure in a big way. The real-life Romeo or Juliet you're looking for will elude you and you will be greatly disappointed. We are all flawed and broken in some way. Don't look for perfection; look for genuine humanity and godliness. Look for someone who has opened their heart to the Savior and loves Him with all their heart, soul, mind, and strength—and is able to love you as they love themselves.

Dating or Courtship?

Dating can be fun, stressful, exciting, and serious business all at the same time. Whether you date a lot or choose the courtship path, it is best to decide your approach before you begin the process. There are pros and cons to both of these plans. Some people believe that you should date a lot of different people along the way. Going from one person to another after another after another may be a waste of valuable time and also potentially hurtful. It can lead to a lot of emotional damage.

Others believe it is more important to go out in groups to really get to know someone first before beginning a "courtship" between just the two of you. This method offers more accountability when it comes to physical temptation. Getting to know someone in a group setting has its benefits. Seeing how they interact with others can be very insightful. But it may also be difficult to know them on a personal level.

The truth is, dating is serious business. It is not to be trifled with, taken for granted, or taken lightly. It is not a game. Dating affects *who you are and who you become.* It will also affect the person(s) you date.

Date Yourself!

That's right, spend some time with yourself. Turn off the phone, the TV, the Xbox, the PS3 or 4 or 5. . .and get into the quiet and sit with yourself. Listen to what is in your heart. What thoughts are roaming through your mind? What occupies your thoughts? Identify those things you just can't stop thinking about. Defining those things will tell you a lot about the kind of person you are. It's amazing what you'll discover when you take the time to look inward. Sometimes putting your thoughts down on paper can help clarify what's going on in your head and your heart. Don't worry about what you may write—you can always tear it up and throw it away. But the process of actually putting your thoughts in writing is a great way to discover your inner thoughts, fears, and desires. And that is what makes journaling so important.

Relationships can be difficult. It's very important to find the ones that will build you up and not tear you down. Seek out the people who will make you a better person. Continue to pursue a deeper spiritual walk with God and allow Him to lead you to people of integrity, genuineness, and honesty.

Think of it this way: you are a son or daughter of the King of the universe. Shouldn't you be conducting your life as a royal? Not haughty or stuck-up or self-important or self-righteous, but as the kind of royal who is good, loving, compassionate, merciful, and full of grace, and who brings peace and wisdom to difficult situations. Isn't this also the kind of partner you would like to have by your side? One who makes good decisions and is thoughtful and strong?

As you work toward this goal, ask yourself these important questions to guide your journey inward:

- Have I surrendered my heart to God and invited Him to make me whole?
- Who am I attracted to?
- What is it about this person that attracts me to them?
- What is my motivation for wanting to spend time with this person? Is it only physical attraction?
- What do I see in them that feels like they could heal me or make me feel better about myself?
- What am I expecting to get out of this relation ship? What am I ready to give?
- What are my weaknesses when it comes to the opposite sex?
- How have I been broken or wounded by the opposite sex (this includes a parent)?

- How is that wound/hurt motivating me toward this person?
- What are my hopes and dreams for my future?
- Where does marriage fit into my hopes and dreams?
- What has God said to me about my heart and dreams for the future?
- What do I believe about sex before marriage?
- Who are my role models after whom I would like to pattern my life?
- How would having sex change me?
- How would it change my relationship with God?
- How would it change my relationship with my parents/family?
- How would it improve my life?
- What are the potential dangers? What kind of damage or consequences might result?
- Is it worth it?

So. . .What Are You Looking For?

As you go through the process of figuring out who you are, you will see more clearly what type of person you should be dating. Your list will probably include a lot of internal qualities that align with your own. So it's time to grab your journal and work through the following:

Find a Mentor

Find an adult in your life whom you trust and respect. This can be a parent, older sibling, teacher, pastor, or family friend. Share your list with them and ask if they would be willing to give some honest feedback. Carefully think about what they tell you. Most likely this person is older and can offer some real-world advice that you can use. But it's not always easy.

What about the Chemistry?

Chemistry is that initial magnetic attraction two people feel for one another. It can be quite exciting and make you feel alive. But does it last? And is it a good foundation on which to build a lasting relationship? Not so much. The truth is, people who build their relationships on chemistry alone will soon be disappointed. Yet it's what we see in the movies and on TV and hear in songs. A guy or girl walks into a room and—*bam!*—there's the person they want to be with. Unfortunately, what Hollywood depicts usually ends in heartache and separation, failure and divorce. Chemistry between two people is a good thing. It's just not a strong foundation for long-lasting commitments.

Who's Your Role Model?

Do you know any couples who have a solid relationship? Take a look at these relationships and see what makes them healthy and loving. Ask these couples questions and let them tell you what they have learned. You may be surprised by their answers.

Make a Friend

It may sound cliché. But the best relationships often begin as strong friendships. Who are your friends? Do you have both guy and girl friends? List them along with how long you have known each one. Are they good friends who will stick with you through the hard times? Or are they fair weather friends who will leave you hanging when you are sick, sad, or upset? Real friendship takes time! An old saying says that you should walk with someone through the seasons of joy, sorrow, anger, gladness, and pain before you're sure of their friendship. If someone isn't a strong friend, he or she will never be a strong dating partner. And the same goes for you. Strong relationships are never one sided. Would your friends list you as a solid friend? Any person who is really serious about dating you will respect this process and will also adopt an attitude of wanting to know you much better before starting to get serious.

One of my best friends in the world, Dave, was on

the phone with me while I was going through the drive-through one day. The line was going very slowly, and I started to growl. Very quietly, he said to me, "Tess, you are one of the sweetest people I know. . .but you sure are impatient!" I had to laugh.

He was very respectfully and sweetly helping me to see something about myself that I didn't realize was a problem. He held the mirror up so I could see myself the way I was presenting myself to him. I didn't get offended or angry. I was *grateful* that he was honest with me. It made me love him more as my friend and trust him because he was gentle but truthful with me. The right man or woman will help us be a better person.

The safest way to be sure about the person you're about to start dating is to know them first—as a true friend. But, if you don't know them well, continually ask questions as you get to know them. . .*before* you actually start a dating relationship with them.

As you can see, it takes a lot of effort and energy to both *be* a real person and to *find* a real person. . .not a Hollywood myth. You need to journey with God on the inside and begin the journey to personal wholeness, and at the same time develop a real friendship as the foundation for a long-term relationship with another person.

Desire to be a giver, not just a taker—a blessing, not

just needy. Be mindful of staying within God's will in order to bring peace and joy to your relationship. Find someone who wants to share this journey with you, someone who is also seeking God and His ways.

In the long run, adopting the standards above and staying in process with God, yourself, and the person you want to create a relationship with will result in a stronger you, a stronger them, and perhaps eventually, a stronger "us"!

CHAPTER 6

Seven Secrets Guys Need to Know about Girls

Clue In to What Makes Them Tick

Just one chapter about a girl's secrets? I (Tess) could fill a whole book! Let's start with a great scripture to guide us. It's from the apostle Paul's letter to the believers living in Ephesus (the book of Ephesians in the New Testament):

Watch what God does, and then you do it, like children who learn proper behavior from their parents. Mostly what God does is love you. Keep company with him and learn a life of love. Observe how Christ loved us. His love was not cautious but extravagant. He didn't love in order to get something from us but to give everything of himself to us. Love like that.

Don't allow love to turn into lust, setting off a downhill slide into sexual promiscuity, filthy practices, or bullying greed. Though some tongues just love the taste of gossip, those who follow Jesus have better uses for language than that. Don't talk dirty or silly. That kind of talk doesn't fit our style. Thanksgiving is our dialect. . . .

Out of respect for Christ, be courteously reverent to one another. (5:1–4, 21 MSG)

Paul has a lot to say about marriage. These verses carry many keys to the secret doors of a woman's heart. Now that we have a basis for godly relationships, let's take a closer look at some secrets of a girl's heart and how a young man can find the key to unlocking them.

1. We Need Guys to See Our Inner Beauty

Women are created by God with an exquisite inner beauty. Only God can truly open the heart of a woman. God's desire for us is to show our beauty and uniqueness to the world. This reflects His love and creativity. In order to see a woman's true beauty, a man should have the heart of God for her.

As Paul says in Ephesians, "Christ's love makes the church whole. *His words evoke her beauty.* Everything he does and says is designed to bring the best out of her, dressing her in dazzling white silk, radiant with holiness" (5:25–27 MSG).

The first secret of a woman's heart is discovering her

beauty and cherishing it. As you've probably figured out by now, beauty has little to do with a woman's outward appearance; it's all about her spirit. This takes time, patience, and maturity. But if you care about her, you will make the journey.

2. Guys Who Are Emotionally Strong Are Most Attractive

Whether or not you agree, females are tough. They work hard, they go to school, they do household chores, they meet the needs of their husbands and children, they work in their communities, and they serve God. They bear children and keep the world moving forward.

And as we think about dating relationships—and eventually marriage—we are seeking guys who are strong, who cover us with love, who engage us in good conversation, who listen to us, and who pray for (and with) us.

We want a guy who knows himself and is not insecure in his relationship with God. We want a man who talks to God, listens to Him, and is obedient to the Holy Spirit's guidance. This is strength.

> But the fruit of the Spirit is love, joy, peace, patience, kindness, goodness, faithfulness, gentleness, self-control; against such things there is no law.
> (Galatians 5:22–23 NASB)

Women want a strong partner. Every close relationship and marriage must be based on sharing both our strengths and our weaknesses. Often people in healthy relationships will say that their strengths and weaknesses are well matched: when one partner has a weakness, the other person matches it with their strength.

And He has said to me, "My grace is sufficient for you, for power is perfected in weakness." Most gladly, therefore, I will rather boast about my weaknesses, so that the power of Christ may dwell in me. (2 Corinthians 12:9 NASB)

Power (from God) is made perfect in weakness! God wants us to share our strengths with each other to counteract our areas of weakness. This is what He does for us, and He calls us to do it for one another!

3. We Need to Feel Safe around You

This is an enormous secret to opening the heart of a female: create a safe place for her to be herself! How do you create a safe place? Think of a hawk's nest: the male hawk builds a nest high above the ground in a rock crag or the crown of a tall tree, usually within sight of a body of water. He soars far above the nest and fields, carefully watching for food or predators. Women want to know that a man creates a safe place for her in his life, free from abuse (with words or actions), where she is honored, respected, and accepted just the way she is.

How do you create a safe place for a girl? Here are a few hints:

- Be kind to her and to those around you. Women who see men putting others down, constantly angry, using abusive language, or behaving in an out-of-control manner will not feel safe.

- Respect her. What does this mean? Listen to her, "hear" what she's saying, and be able to take her advice or give her advice based on what you've heard.

- Most of the time, all a woman really wants you to do is *listen*. She'll figure out her next steps herself the majority of the time. Being able to talk it out with you will help her process and come to a conclusion.

- Don't try to fix her. Remember, you both have strengths and weaknesses. God is the only "fixer" when it comes to our hearts and spirits. Point her to Jesus! Ask the Holy Spirit to speak to her heart!

- Give constructive criticism only when asked. The *best* way to do this is to ask questions with genuine curiosity. Do this with respect, gentleness, and the truth spoken in love.

• Never, ever, ever, ever strike or physically harm a woman. Protect her from anyone who tries. If you are leaving an event in separate cars, walk her to her car and don't leave until she pulls out. Stay there to see that her car starts and her doors are locked and she drives away safely. If you are walking down the street, keep her on the inside away from traffic. Open and close her car door for her. Your desire to protect her will make her feel safe.

• Never abuse her with your words. If you disagree, state your case intelligently. Be a mature man of God and disagree, but discuss things reasonably. A lively argument can be good for a relationship!

• Believe me, we women beat ourselves up a lot already because we tend to be *very* aware of our shortcomings and faults. Never call someone dumb, ugly, ignorant, or stupid. Women will never feel safe with a man who can't argue with them intelligently with a spirit of discovery.

4. Faith in Jesus Means Everything to Us

Any godly young woman who loves Jesus with all her heart is looking for a godly young man who is doing the same.

You can't lead where you haven't traveled. You won't know the road. Prepare to be a great godly husband and dad *now*! You don't just wake up one day and—*bam!*—you're there!

Dive into your relationship with Jesus. Ask the Holy Spirit daily to create a clean heart within you and renew your spirit and teach you His song. By falling in love with Jesus first, you will have His heart within you to truly love a woman the way God created her to be loved.

Allow the Holy Spirit to search your heart. Allow Him to reveal to you wounds inflicted by others, and invite Him to heal you and make you whole. Sometimes this may involve receiving counseling from someone older in the faith who has wisdom. But many times the Holy Spirit will give you wisdom directly and show you the way to become free from bondages to sin, slavery to addictions (such as porn), and anger and hurt from old wounds.

This takes time. Be honest with the woman you are getting to know if some of these hurts and wounds threaten to undermine or destroy your relationship. This brings us to the next key. . .

5. Accountability Is Key

If there are things in your life that threaten to destroy your relationship (or worse, your life), then be accountable for them. Get counseling. Be honest. Work on healing those wounds. Don't beat yourself up about them or have unrealistic ideas about how fast you should heal. Give yourself time. Allow God to work and allow others you respect, who are kind, gentle, truthful, and wise to speak into your life. Follow their advice.

Read God's Word and allow the Holy Spirit to teach you and lead you. Listen to Him speak to your spirit, and take baby steps to follow Him.

A girl needs to know that her boy is accountable to God, that he admits to his mistakes and shortcomings or sin, and that he is honestly and genuinely working every day to be a better person.

A guy who is prideful, resists counseling, or refuses to admit when he is wrong or hurtful is *not* the kind of man any self-respecting woman will ever stay with. Even if it takes you years to work on your issues, do it!

Girls want a "spiritually healthy" man to partner with them and lead their home.

6. Guys—Learn to Cherish Us!

Girls love to be enjoyed, cherished, and included in your life. Find creative ways to include us in your thoughts and plans. A girl who feels desired will open her heart to you when she sees she is important enough to be included in your activities and important events in your life.

Discover her interests and join in on the fun. It's okay to be silly and willing to do crazy stuff. Be spontaneous, or surprise her by making plans that include her interests.

Also, ask her to hang out with you and your friends. It's good when the people in your life get to know each other. She needs to see you in the context of your "normal" life to get perspective on who you really are.

Just enjoy being together. Laugh! Have fun! Be active! Get to know girls in a spirit of adventure. And leave having sex out of it.

7. We Want the Right Kind of Intimacy

Several years ago a brochure was published for teenagers called *101 Ways to Make Love without Doing It!* It was pretty clever. The list of 101 ways to romance another person was actually created by teenagers! The essence of the brochure was to find ways to create intimacy and trust and to deepen relationship and romance without actually having sex. It included everything from going on a hike together to serving at a community soup kitchen.

Guys and girls approach and define *intimacy* in different ways. From a female's point of view, being intimate with a guy means that he keeps our secrets, he listens and understands our deepest fears and desires, he knows our vulnerabilities and protects them. Can you think of ways you can develop intimacy with a girl with these expectations in mind? Hugging, kissing, and having sex have nothing to do with it. In fact, making love is much, much more than sex.

Making love involves the whole person. (More on this later in the book.) How can you truly make love to someone you don't know? How can you completely give your whole self to someone if you don't know who you are or who they are? Girls want a guy who appreciates true intimacy.

God teaches us that we become "one" in the sacrament of marriage. And in the oneness, we are free to explore the benefits of a physical relationship. But that "oneness" starts long before we are married. It starts in our hearts and our minds as we get to know each other. Guys, reveal your hearts to us.

CHAPTER 7

Seven Secrets Girls Need to Know about Guys

Clue In to How They're Wired

Questions. Tons of them are swirling around that brain of yours: *What makes some guys cool conversationalists while others freeze up when a girl says hi? How is it that they're fun to be around one minute. . .and then become insensitive jerks? (Like when they get around other guys.) Is there only one thing on every boy's mind: "scoring"—with sports and with girls? Do they ever outgrow juvenile behavior?*

Obviously, you've figured out that boys are different from you—and that's a good thing! Yet they're not simply different on the outside; they're unique *inside*, too. The male gender thinks and reacts to situations in very different ways from you. So, what's a girl to do? How can you figure out what he's thinking. . .and eventually connect with him?

If you're feeling frustrated, take a deep breath and relax.

I (Michael) have filled this chapter with the essential tips, advice, and secrets that guys really *do* want you to know but would never tell you on their own. And they not only want you to *know* what I'm about to share, but they want you to truly understand it.

So grab a soda and start reading. . . .

1. "Most Guys Are 'All about the Eyes'"

You've probably heard this a million times before, but I need to make it one million and one times: guys are visual, girls connect through emotions. It's really important that you understand this.

Visually, it just doesn't take much for a guy to get turned on by a girl. Teen boys like the way you look. They like your shape, your scent, even the sound of your voice. God created males to be this way. (True, our culture, trauma, and other factors have messed this up for some guys, but we'll save that discussion for another book.) Generally speaking, it's pretty easy for you to catch a boy's attention. This is both a good thing and a not-so-good thing.

Sadly, too many girls confuse (or abuse) this. Likewise, too many guys make wrong decisions based on sight and physical attraction instead of actually getting to know a girl. It's time for both genders to take responsibility for their actions.

First, don't send the wrong signals by reeling in a guy with your looks, when what you really want is friendship and emotional intimacy. The apostle Paul gave this instruction: "I also want the women to dress modestly, with decency and propriety, adorning themselves, not with elaborate hairstyles or gold or pearls or expensive clothes, but with good deeds, appropriate for women who profess to worship God" (1 Timothy 2:9–10 NIV).

Second, make every effort to have self-control and to guard your heart. "For the grace of God has appeared that offers salvation to all people. It teaches us to say 'No' to ungodliness and worldly passions, and to live self-controlled, upright and godly lives in this present age, while we wait for the blessed hope—the appearing of the glory of our great God and Savior, Jesus Christ, who gave himself for us to redeem us from all wickedness and to purify for himself a people that are his very own, eager to do what is good" (Titus 2:11–14 NIV).

2. "Think of Me as a Poet-Warrior: I'm Both Sensitive *and* Aggressive"

Every guy has a soft side. This includes artists, geeks, jocks, hunters, mechanics—boys from every walk of life and with every personality type. Most enjoy music and "fancy" food. Some cry during heart-tugging movies. And nearly every guy loves to create things with his hands—whether it's a special dish for that special girl or a wooden side table for Mom.

But in case you hadn't noticed, he has an aggressive side, too. It's as if his inner jerk takes over at times, and he becomes highly self-centered. During those moments, he struggles to express and process his changing moods. He may even default to physical outbursts.

Why?

First, let's go back in time—actually, all the way back to the sixteenth through twenty-sixth weeks of fetal development.

Sometime during this stage, God "masculinized" the infant boy's brain with testosterone so he could one day "think like a man." The result: testosterone destroyed millions of fiber optic–like connections between his left-brain speech center and his right-brain feelings-emotions-beliefs region. Here's how the process is explained by Donald M. Joy, PhD, professor of Human Development and Christian Education at Asbury Theological Seminary:

> *Several interesting things happened to a boy's fetal brain as he was being created in his mother's womb. The mother's androgens combined with testosterone from the baby's developing testicles to form a frost-like,*

chemical coating on the entire left hemisphere of the boy's brain. The coating is God's way of "masculinizing" a boy. Consequently, men are able to "focus in" and give intense attention to anything, almost without distraction.[1]

Dr. Joy says this is why most guys have a tougher time putting their thoughts and feelings into words. It's also why teen boys release emotions through intense, energetic bursts: they fly off the handle, slam doors, beat their fists on a wall, lash out at their siblings. Then they shut down and retreat into some sort of focused activity, such as a computer game. (If you have teenage brothers, I'm sure you've witnessed this.)

There's one more fact you need to understand: testosterone fuels a guy's appetite for sex—and is the force behind his apparent obsession with this subject. It's one of the reasons why husbands pursue their wives. Did God make a mistake here? Not at all! It's actually a very cool part of our Creator's amazing design. Yet the Lord requires that every male—from adolescence to manhood—develop a system of self-control over his sexuality and express that energy *only* in a committed marriage relationship. (See 1 Thessalonians 4:3–5 and reread Titus 2:11–14.) In this relationship, women are protected and guys become healthier, more fulfilled people.

So if a boy tries to convince you that having sex is how couples share their love for each other, you know better. (It's the sex on his brain that's talking.) Tell him that sex is designed for marriage, point him to the verses above. . .and then cut him loose.

3. "My Ego Is Fragile in Spite of a Tough Exterior"

Guys are marshmallow-filled armadillos. It's true. Some of them try to act cool and tough on the outside because that's how our culture (and other guys) define manhood. But there's a good chance that inside they're hurting, the same way girls do. And while they often struggle to express themselves—remember our conversation above—guys are trying to work through all kinds of conflicting emotions.

Here's something else to keep in mind: all it takes is for one person to make fun of him and he can be ruined for the rest of the day. One poorly timed slam and he may end up feeling like he's dying inside. That's why girls should never make fun of a boy's looks—just as he should never criticize yours. The one person on the face of the planet he desperately wants to impress is *you*. Tell him he's creepy, geeky, or ugly and—*bam!*—his ego is crushed.

Case-in-point: Fifteen-year-old Logan had a medium build and average looks. But his older sister teased him by calling him ugly. "Hi, ugly. Want to go get a burger with me?" "Hey, ugly! Where's the remote?" This went on for years. And even though Logan knew his sister loved him, he never felt attractive to the opposite sex until he was in a relationship with a wonderful Christian girl in college who consistently affirmed him.[2]

My advice: do your best to build up, encourage, and affirm the guys in your life. If a boy dresses well, tell him! Say things like, "Hey, your hair looks nice today!" Let him know that he has your acceptance.

4. "Sometimes I Don't Talk Much, but I Hear You"

Let's head back to point 2 and how some guys struggle to express themselves. Studies indicate that women use thirty thousand to fifty thousand words, while men use only twenty thousand to twenty-five thousand. Incredible, isn't it? The fact is, women are able to outtalk men and even seem to have an innate need to share *everything* they're thinking. Guys, on the other hand, can process things inwardly and be happy never to voice what they've just thought through.

So don't freak out over moments of silence or those times when he doesn't want to open up about what he's thinking. He's probably not mad or trying to hide something from you. It's just the way his brain works.

At the same time, don't let his lack of words fool you. He actually hears you much more than you realize. That's why it's important for you to carefully weigh your words, what you say and how you say it. Remember fifteen-year-old Logan—the boy we talked about above?

So with these two insights in mind, the key to solid connections with the guys in your life involves finding common ground. (Flip back to chapter 4 for a more thorough discussion.) Is the boy you're getting to know a poet or a writer? A musician? An athlete? Focus on his interests—the things in his life that seem to define him—and use these things to formulate door openers. Begin with easy, fun, nonthreatening statements and questions, letting him fill in the blanks, so to speak: "When did you start writing songs?" "What inspires you to write?" "Is this a hobby or something that will turn into your future career?"

Tuning in on what he likes and how he communicates—whether it's behind a mic, on the court, or on the stage—will help you connect with him. Take an active interest in every area of his life. Before you know it, he'll be using more words than you. Actually, scratch that last part. There's no way that he'll ever use more words than you. (Kidding, of course!)

5. "I Want a Girlfriend Who Is Close to God"

Listen to the heart of seventeen-year-old Daniel:

I really want to be a man of God and follow His will for my life. The events of last summer solidified this desire in me. (I guess I needed a spiritual nudge!) Let me tell you about it.

I went on a missions trip to a camp were they bus kids from a city called Coatsville, Pennsylvania. Every day during the summer, Christians get them away from the horrible environment of drugs and violence and teach them the hope of Jesus.

Getting involved with this ministry changed my life. I've come to realize that I can't run from God anymore, and I can't ignore Him. I was spiritually dead, and now I am growing. So pray for me and pray for those little children.

God changed Daniel's life through that ministry experience. He's on fire now, and he's ready to let Jesus change the world through him. As far as relationships go, having a healthy, growing connection with the Lord is Daniel's number one priority. What about having a girlfriend? Of course he wants that, too, "but only if she's made Jesus the priority of her life."

Want a godly guy? Take Daniel's advice: *be a godly girl*. Before you even think about having a relationship with a boy, make time to fully develop an intimate relationship with Jesus. Walk your talk, share your faith, and encourage your male friends to become men after God's own heart. How? Invite them to a campus Bible study group, invite them to your youth group, keep them in your prayers, reach out to them when they hurt. The sky's the limit on what you can do.

6. "My World Can Feel So Brutal"

A guy's world often looks and feels a lot like yours. Like you. . .

• he must survive a climate that in one moment is playful and childlike then suddenly changes to harsh, overwhelming, and cruel.

• he knows that popularity is measured by how well he does with the opposite sex.

• he feels that rejection is a fate worse than death.

• he is fascinated by those strange creatures known as "the opposite sex."

• he can't even control his own emotions from minute to minute.

And just as you are becoming a woman—and are trying to figure out what that means—most guys feel very confused about what real masculinity is all about. Their parents and the church tell them one thing, their friends say something different, and the media often paints a picture that's impossible to live up to. Here's how one expert sums up the issue: "A large proportion of young males view drinking and having sexual conquests as the appropriate way to begin to prove they are an adult male. Their male peers are saying, 'Be tough,' and girls are saying, 'Tell me about your feelings.'"[3]

For more insight into the guys' world, take a look at what these young men told me:

Brad, 16: "It's as if guys are expected to be macho clones, and I'm sick of it. At school, I have to put on this stupid tough-guy armor and be who the crowd says I should be. I wish I could just be myself. If I'm not the bully, I become the bullied."

Weston, 15: "The world of teen guys can be a scary jungle. If we show any kind of weakness, we're hunted down and destroyed by 'alpha' males. Tough guys prey on the weak."

Shane, 17: "You'd think guys in the church would be different—but often they aren't. Even Christian males are scared inside. We put on acts and copy the world. I want to be different! I want to start being the man God created me to be."

Devon, 16: "I don't feel like I fit in anywhere. I look in the mirror, and I don't even know who I am. I look around school, even my youth group, and all I see are cliques and clones. The so-called 'cool kids' only hang out with other 'cool clones.' And if you don't measure up, life is cruel."

Ian, 15: "Sometimes I feel lost, lonely, and forgotten. At other times, I feel as if every eye is on *me*—like I'm the featured act in today's teenage freak show!"

Steven, 14: "Teen guys are so messed up. I know because I am one. If you don't look, talk, and act a certain way, you're constantly picked on. Life is hell for guys—and parents and teachers are clueless."

7. "I Need Time in My 'Cave'"

Every guy needs his alone time. Maybe it's time alone in the garage to tinker with an engine. Or perhaps he wants time alone to lift weights in the spare bedroom.

He needs time in the sanity and safety of his "cave" so he can face the insanity of the real world. Come to think of it, girls need this, too. So don't be upset when he wants to be alone. Give him some space.

Let him retreat to his cave—so he can sort through a problem.

Let him talk when he's ready. If you sense that he's trying to work through a personal problem, communicate that you are available to lend an ear.

Let him open up at his own pace. Never prod him to cough up every detail. This could cause him to shut down even more.

Let him know that his feelings are safe with you. This last step is crucial for every couple and for every relationship—from the dating kind to marriages to parent-kid relationships. It must be nurtured by both guys and girls through an attitude of acceptance.

CHAPTER 8

The Impact of Sexual Sin on Your Dating Life

Been There, Done That (and I Wish I Hadn't)

Is it possible to know more and less at the same time? Our culture is saturated with sex. Everywhere we look we are bombarded with images and messages about sex. You would think that this would lead to a better understanding of the origin, purpose, and consequences of "going there" physically. And in some ways, maybe we are more knowledgeable. We are becoming very familiar with the human body. And it's not just because of the constant flow of Internet porn. It's now a normal part of many TV shows. You know the ones that have people cooking, dating, and even surviving while wearing absolutely nothing? That computer-generated blur that covers their private parts is almost laughable. And it leaves nothing up to the imagination. But all this really does is make us focus on the outward physical image of the person. It is communicating that we should decide a person's worth by their appearance. In this way, we haven't developed a better understanding of sex at all. We have lessened the importance of all the other parts of sex. We have traded a beautiful thing for a quick and easy fix. So much so, most young men and women have this unrealistic expectation that sex is somehow *required* in order to be in a relationship. Where did that come from?

This expectation was the product of a cultural "revolution" that occurred in the 1960s and 1970s that declared people wanted to be free of the expectations of right and wrong and to be able to live any way they wanted to as long as they didn't think they were hurting anybody else.

It was a cultural revolution that started out sounding like a good idea, but actually resulted in many casualties from drug abuse, illicit sex, abortions, unwanted children, sexually transmitted disease, broken hearts and lives, and the abandonment of many social "rules" that kept young people safe in their dating relationships. This was never the purpose of sex. It was meant to be a pleasurable and intimate way for two people to bond with one another. This is not the type of bond to share with the world. It was designed for couples in lifelong relationships that have been solidified by marriage. This may not be a quick and easy feel-good fix. But it is the original intent of sex. And in this type of setting, there is a lot of freedom and enjoyment.

The expectation of "no sex before marriage" came from the Christian principles embraced by many Americans since the birth of our nation. And until the "cultural and sexual revolution" in the 1960s and '70s, everyone agreed with no sex before marriage because it went against God's desire and will for His people. Those principles served to protect our hearts from brokenness, deep wounds, and spiritual harm, and our bodies from disease.

The Christian principles that served to protect our hearts, spirits, minds, and bodies began to disappear from our culture and were replaced by the freedom and acceptance for people to live life any way they wanted to, including taking drugs, smoking, drinking, having sex, cursing, and being dishonest and self-centered. The slogan became "If it feels good, do it!" without regard to the consequences and damage being done or with any thought for the future.

Expectations

Stop pretending that you are not influenced by everyone else's expectations when it comes to sex. Sex is not free from consequences. We may live in a culture that promotes sexual freedom, but only when it fits into their definition.

It's time to step back and recognize that your basic beliefs about you and your body are being influenced every day by social expectations. They are delivered to you through your friends, the Internet, movies, TV, books, and maybe even your boyfriend or girlfriend. It can be confusing and complicated. And this makes it all too easy to give in to temporary pleasure and join the crowd.

The prospect of physical contact with someone you really like and want to create a relationship with can be emotionally overwhelming. Expectations are usually high, and you may have wondered, *Why am I waiting?* After all, if everyone else is doing it, then is it really that big of a deal?

Will You Conform?

Why should we conform to this culture? Many times it's to avoid painful rejection, being left out of circles of friends who may think we're weird for our choices. But will these people be there for you the rest of your life while you deal with the potentially harmful consequences of your actions? Or will they walk away when life gets messy and the going gets tough?

What if you get a sexually transmitted disease? What if you and your partner get pregnant? What if your peers begin to abuse you or hurt you if you don't do what they want? Where will your close circle of friends be then?

Even if they do stick with you, what can they really do to help you heal? Your friends are just as clueless as you.

Make a Decision to Stand

You must start *now* to stand on your own two feet, decide who you are and what kind of life you choose for yourself. "Above all else, guard your heart, for everything you do flows from it" (Proverbs 4:23 NIV).

Knowing that there is great pressure to conform to this current code of sexual behavior means it's extra hard to resist. Therefore, it is vital to enter into relationships knowing who we are and what we believe.

Diving into the deep end of the pool without first learning to swim is a recipe for suicide, so why would you do it with your heart and your future? Are you so desperate for love and attention that you are willing to possibly sacrifice your future to have temporary satisfaction now? Does that make sense in the long run?

Here's what the New Testament scriptures say about that:

Romans 8:8, 13 NLT: Those who are still under the control of their sinful nature can never please God. . . . For if you live by its dictates, you will die. But if through the power of the Spirit you put to death the deeds of your sinful nature, you will live.

1 Corinthians 6:18 NLT: Run from sexual sin! No other sin so clearly affects the body as this one does. For sexual immorality is a sin against your own body.

1 Thessalonians 4:3–4 NIV: It is God's will that you should be sanctified: that you should avoid sexual immorality; that each of you should learn to control your own body in a way that is holy and honorable.

Hebrews 13:4 NIV: Marriage should be honored by all, and the marriage bed kept pure, for God will judge the adulterer and all the sexually immoral.

So, What Made You Do It?

There are usually four reasons why people enter into sexual relationships:

Desire and a Longing for Love

A beautiful young woman I (Tess) know couldn't wait to get away from home. It wasn't that she was mistreated or didn't have a loving home. She had the heart of an adventurer that her single mom had instilled in her. But she never had the love of a loving Dad growing up. She didn't date in high school and was kind of a geeky girl—not exactly cheerleader material. Growing up, she would rather watch the science channel than go shopping.

But when she took her first trip away from home with several friends on a "missions" trip to a Third World country for several weeks, she met and "fell in love" with a handsome young man who was working with them. One thing led to another and my beautiful young friend succumbed to the overwhelming feeling of being loved by a man, and they had sex.

Promises were made. Promises were broken. And nine months later she had a beautiful baby. Unmarried with no job and unable to afford child care and college, she had to take part-time jobs to care for her young child.

Her life, so full of hopes and dreams for college and a career as a scientist, became defined not by what she was but by what she wasn't. She went through depression and hardship. She is a great mom and very loving, but her dreams were shattered because she did not know herself enough to have a plan before beginning a relationship.

The Hole in Your Heart

Perhaps the person you're attracted to wants to move into a more physical relationship. You may feel really attracted to them and want to have them all to yourself. You believe they are "the one," and this will be the love that lasts a lifetime. But how can that be with no commitment? Loving someone in the moment, especially when you are young, is not a lifetime commitment.

Your desire to be intimately connected to another human being may be an attempt to fill a hole in your life. Maybe your heart is searching for completion and you hope to gain that through physical intimacy. But sex does not equal intimacy at all. Intimacy is the deepest level of relationship that takes time and vulnerability. It grows out of knowing and trusting someone over time. And only with time can you really know if a person is trustworthy, honorable, and completely devoted to you. Sex does not result in that kind of intimacy. Actually, the opposite is true. You give away a little bit of your soul every time you have sex. And when that little bit walks away with each partner, it leaves an even bigger hole in your heart.

Fear

If you fear the stigma of not having sex, then you have bought into the cultural myth. It's the one that tells you that you are less if you are sexually inexperienced. It may influence you to give in to pressure from friends who may tease you and laugh at you if you're not active. Or maybe you are afraid that you will lose your relationship if you don't "take it to the next level." Again, these ideas are fueled by people who have given in to the pressure themselves and want you to join them. They may be trying to lessen their own regrets.

Rebellion

A fourth reason people may enter into a sexual relationship is rebellion. The root of rebellion is anger. If someone is angry at their parents or friends or not happy with their life, they may throw caution to the wind and break all the rules, getting involved in sex, drugs, alcohol and partying, and rejecting their faith. We've all seen people who don't seem to have any reason for acting out; they just don't want anyone to tell them how to live their life. They set no limits and live for the moment.

This kind of rebellion usually comes because of broken dreams or unmet expectations. Things don't turn out the way they want, their heart is torn, their spirit is broken, or their expectations aren't met by their family, friends, God, or their community, so they run as hard as they can in the opposite direction.

Sexual relationships with these kinds of people only end one way: in danger, hurt, and heartache. Stay away! At first, rebellious people seem strong and independent; they may seem mysterious and brooding. Certain types of young men and women who have a need to "fix" other people, to be their savior, will rush to "save" them. Don't be codependent. No one has ever been saved by sex.

In the end, rebellious people will often "love 'em and leave 'em." Don't get left and hurt by one of these people! Steer clear! If you find yourself constantly drawn to people you feel a need to "save," then you are quite possibly headed for a codependent relationship. Examine why you have this need in your life. You will be ready for a relationship when you are able to stand on your own two feet while expecting your love interest to do the same. This is the type of maturity needed for a relationship to last a lifetime.

Four Reasons to Steer Clear of Sexual Sin

The results of sin are as unique to each person as their fingerprints. "If only I had thought about the consequences" is the comment we often hear from those who have gone too far sexually. So what is the impact of sexual sin? Take a look:

The Impact: Distance

First and foremost, we know that sin in our lives can push us further away from God. Not because He moves away from us, but because we choose to move away from Him. Has this happened to you? Have you engaged in some sort of sin and then ran away from God because you didn't want to have to face Him with it?

There is a remedy for that. It is called humble repentance. (We will talk more about that in chapter 11, "But

I've Already Blown It—What Now?") There is a way to close the gap and renew your relationship with the Love of your life—Jesus.

The Impact: A Wound

Sin also creates wounds in our hearts, eventually leaving us cold and alone and feeling rejected—especially if we feel that God has abandoned us. But again, *He never leaves us* or forsakes us. He does not abandon us. We must run to Him and talk it out, open our hearts to His love and forgiveness and accept a new start. He can heal the wounds in our hearts before they leave nasty scars that will affect all of our future relationships—not just with the opposite sex, but also with family, friends, and our faith community.

The Impact: Ripple Effects

The Bible tells us that we are all connected in the body of Christ. And if one of us hurts, we all hurt. If one of us sins, it somehow affects the whole body of Christ. Even though you may not perceive the effects, sin has a ripple effect in the spiritual life of the whole body. When we sin, we actually sin against our own bodies, against another person, and against God. Everyone is affected even if they don't realize it.

This is a big reason why we should never harbor "secret

sins" in our lives. It is no secret to God, of course, but the fact that sin makes room for darkness to have a foothold in our lives means that darkness also enters the body of Christ through us. That is a big deal. When you enter into a sinful sexual relationship with someone, you are affecting the community of believers.

The Impact: Generational Curses

Another thing to consider is that even though you are young, the life you lead now creates a legacy for your future children. Even though you are not thinking that far ahead, they will inherit your spiritual legacy someday. Do you want that legacy to be one filled with poor choices, bad consequences, and separation from God?

We can see the results of these "generational curses" all around us. For example, 75 percent of children who are raised in a household of smokers will become smokers themselves by age sixteen. That is a culture of cancer and death that gets passed along. Children raised by parents of divorce are much likelier to divorce themselves, and children raised by parents who were abused are likelier to be abused. Children live out what they learn at home.

Think about this when considering the kind of person you want to marry. Have you thought about what "curses" or "blessings" in their lives they may carry forward into your relationship? Are they addicted to pornography? Do they carry the shame of disease from a life of partying? Do they already have children from previous relationships? Do they keep their promises and stay true to their word? Or do they shirk responsibility and avoid accountability? These are "curses" and "blessings" that will be passed down to your children. Look at the reality of the "now," because in many cases it will prophesy the "not yet."

The Good News

A good friend of mine got pregnant at an early age and had two children by a man who was very abusive. When she finally got the courage to leave, she was destitute and had nowhere to live and found it hard to feed her children. One of her children was taken away from her and put in another home. Over the next several years, she was rarely allowed to see the child.

My friend cried tears for years and years because she had lost her child. But as she gave her heart to Jesus and began to trust Him with her child's future, God assured her that one day her child would grow up and want to know her again. She prayed that both her and her daughter's wounds would be healed and their relationship would be restored through His love. Right now, as you read this, God is doing it. But it has taken a lot of years, heartache, regret, prayer, and tears. God is faithful to restore what we have lost. But our heart can really hurt in the process.

The good news is that no matter where we are in life, God can wipe our slate clean and give us a new start and create in us a new legacy. He can go before us and create a new future for us and our future family. He can restore us over time as we walk with Him and love Him.

For Your Consideration

Consider the real foundation of your life and your joy. Think about the solid foundation that God has given to all of us so we can build beautiful, respectful, passionate, purposeful, and solid relationships.

Sex outside of marriage is *not* required for intimacy or staying together. *Ever*. And no "date" should ever have that expectation placed upon it. Dating is not for consummating relationships or "sealing the deal" to give you bragging rights. This is totally upside down from reality!

Sex becomes a "hook" that people use to try and get what they want out of a relationship. For some, that means a heightened status among their friends; for others it simply boils down to a means of improving their own self-esteem and feeling loved. Some people feel having sex with someone means they are mature, more adult, more *valid* in society, since society expects it of us.

Don't fall for the lie. Just don't do it. Don't get involved too young. It's not healthy. Don't be afraid to say no. What you need to realize is, if you truly love someone, sex can wait. It is a very special and sacred act that God made for marriage.

The Revolution

It's time for another *revolution*! It's time for us to rebel against the unrealistic and harmful expectations of the culture around us. Determine in your heart not to become emotionally/physically involved with someone who does not walk with Jesus. The scriptures are clear: God intends for us to only be joined with another person who loves and walks with Him.

God wants us to share in the deepest intimacy possible as two people joined with Him as "one" in holy marriage. This kind of intimacy is higher and more sacred than we can imagine!

However, intimacy accentuated by God's presence is impossible when the partners are not united spiritually in and by Him. Second Corinthians 6:14 from *The Message* says it this way: "Don't become partners with those who reject God. How can you make a partnership out of right and wrong? That's not partnership; that's war."

The New International Version says it this way: "Do

not be yoked together with unbelievers." What does that mean? When it comes to guy/girl relationships and, ultimately, to marriage, it's important to choose someone who loves and is fully committed to Jesus as a lifelong partner.

What's more, the impact of sin on your dating and relationships is huge. Ripples from your choices flow out into your future and can cause great damage. At the time we choose to sin, the ripples seem very small and without any great effect.

But over time, those ripples can cause a tsunami that can destroy your options, your vision, and your plans for the future. Be aware: choices can take on a life of their own after you release them into the universe. Only God is capable of catching them and transforming them.

There will always be consequences of sin. Jesus died on the cross to take the consequence of death for us, because that's always how sin plays out—it causes the death of something. But God can give our life back and walk with us through the ripples and help us bear the consequences whether they are emotional, spiritual, mental, or physical. He is *for us* and wants us to live victorious lives.

CHAPTER 9

Setting Smart Boundaries and Realistic Goals with the Opposite Sex

Preplan Your Responses before You Get in a Tight Spot

The Way We Were. . .

1970: So there you are, sitting in a car with your date, and you know the moment has arrived for the good-night kiss. You've been anticipating this all night, and you make a little small talk about what a fun (great, awesome, cool, etc.) night it was. You're making eye contact, waiting for the other person to lean in. . .but neither of you does.

Suddenly your mind is filled with anxiety. *Why isn't he [she] kissing me? Maybe they're just not that into me. What did I do wrong? Oh my, this is terrible! I've spent the whole evening thinking she [he] was into me, but maybe I've been wrong this whole time! What am I going to do? Okay, I'm just going to say good-bye and leave.*

So you smile and say, "Well, it's been a good night. I had a great time. Thank you so much. I'll talk to you soon."

And you leave with an awkward smile on your face and a knot in the pit of your stomach. You feel ashamed that you weren't somehow attractive enough or "good enough" to be your date's object of affection.

2014: So there you are, sitting in a car with your date. They lean over and put their hand on your knee and begin to slide it upward. You know you're not ready for this, but you also know that if you stop it will probably create an awkward situation. In the moment, it may be easier to go with what feels good. You feel wanted as your body reacts to the other person. You try to think, but you are too pre-occupied by the touching and kissing.

But, at some point, it gets to be too much and you know you just can't do it. There's a knot in the pit of your stomach as your mind races. You think to yourself, *What am I going to do? How do I get out of this?* You push away and say, "I'm so sorry, I guess I'm just not ready." You apologize for letting it go that far as you pull yourself together and exit the car. As you walk into your house, you know there is a good chance you will never hear from your date again. The last ten minutes just placed you in the "too much drama" category.

What do these two very different scenarios have in common?

The Now and the Not Yet

Sex feels good. And after we hit a certain age, our bodies are drawn to physical gratification. We are surrounded by a culture that pursues instant pleasure with a very casual attitude. Throw in a boyfriend or girlfriend whom you are attracted to and you have a moral dilemma. That's right. It's a moral dilemma. If you pay attention to scripture, your parents, pastors, and a long list of experts, then you know that the effects of sex last much longer that the immediate moment.

Once you begin a physical relationship with someone, you have started down a path full of choices and consequences. But if you head down that road without a plan, then there are many pitfalls that can trip you up. Like a diver swimming with the sharks without a proper plan and safeguards, you could get eaten alive. You'll sustain wounds and scars on your heart, mind, and body that you may have to carry for the rest of your life. Even getting close to having sex can have big, life-altering consequences.

It's important to preplan what you will do when you are faced with certain intimate situations *before* things get too hot and heavy.

What's the Big Deal?

Sex is great in the right setting. And that right setting is a lifelong commitment within a marriage. Participating

MICHAEL ROSS AND TESS COX

in sex outside of marriage opens up your soul, spirit (heart), and body to dangerous influence and harm in the long and short run. Several scriptures deal with sex outside of marriage (for example, Exodus 20:14; Matthew 5:27–30; 1 Corinthians 6:15–20; 7:2, 9; and 1 Thessalonians 4:3–8).

The Bible tells us that when two people have sex they become "one flesh." That means your spirits intermingle and you each get part of the other person. This is a joining of both the physical and spiritual parts of your lives. They become part of you and you become part of them. You both gain and lose.

This is powerful. In God's plan sex is much more than just a recreational activity as some people think. And it is never a casual thing! It's very serious. "It creates a deep, powerful bond—sort of a relational superglue."[1]

Have you ever gotten superglue on your skin? Especially if it's stuck between your fingers? If you have, you know that the superglue is so powerful that in order to separate your two fingers, you will have to lose some skin when you pull them apart.

On a much grander and more serious scale, the same is true for having sex. Yes, it creates a powerful bond between people. But if you are not committed to one another forever in the bonds of marriage, then when you separate from one another and break up, that person leaves with part of you inside them. You have less of "you" to offer someday when you finally meet the person you want to spend the rest of your life with.

Can you imagine what would happen if you had sex with a lot of different people? Someday, when you've finally found the "one" you want to spend the rest of your life with, how much of "you" will be left to give?

If you have sex over and over again, you are literally giving pieces of your spirit away. Why would you do that to yourself? Why would you sabotage your future marriage in this way? Staying true to your faith and waiting to give yourself to that life commitment is worth it!

As you can clearly see, casual sex whether you're fourteen or twenty-four can have serious, long-term effects on your life. Besides the spiritual effects, there are also the unwanted physical risks: HIV, unwanted pregnancy, herpes, gonorrhea, and human papilloma virus (HPV), which can lead to cancer. So it pays to be prepared for the pressure and temptation before you are faced with it.

So, What to Do? You Have to Have a Plan

Dating can be like swimming with the sharks. Setting smart boundaries to protect yourself and realistic goals with the opposite sex *before* you get into a deeper relationship with them is like the diver's suit that protects you as you dive into deep and dangerous waters where sharks swim. To dive in where there is danger of hurt and harm without an escape plan, a good oxygen supply, a lifeline, and some protection is foolish—and somebody's going to get hurt, and probably not the shark!

Preplanning your responses *before* you get into a tight spot is wisdom. The Bible has many verses that speak of using wisdom and getting wisdom. This is where wisdom begins: being alert and opening your eyes to see what is happening around you. Look into your heart and also the motivations of the one with whom you desire to create a deep relationship. What do you see there? Respect? Trust? Patience? Or urgency? Anxiety? Pressure?

Let's look at some practical tools you can use to set smart boundaries and realistic goals with the opposite sex when developing a relationship.

The Toolbox

The first place to start is with *you*! God is already preparing you and giving you the tools you need to be strong in challenging situations. Let's look at some of them.

Tool #1: Know yourself.

This is the most important tool. Know your own *value*. God has placed a very high value on your life. You are precious to Him, and He dreams a great dream for your life. God sees you, loves you, and values you; you should see yourself as His son or daughter and value your life accordingly.

Time is constantly moving forward. Nothing stays the same. Yet God goes before us in time and prepares the way for us, so if we are following Him, our path will be straight and His dream for us will be a great adventure. So value yourself because you are highly valued and greatly loved by God!

In the scriptures, God says to Jeremiah: "I the LORD search the heart and examine the mind, to reward each person according to their conduct, according to what their deeds deserve" (Jeremiah 17:10 NIV). God searches our hearts and minds and digs deep inside us to bring out all the goodness, gifts, and grace He has hidden there. If we take that journey with Him, we will begin to discover all the good things about ourselves and believe in ourselves. He says, "I will give you hidden treasures, riches stored in secret places" (Isaiah 45:3 NIV).

Tool #2: Grow deep roots and be flexible.

Even as young adults, we sometimes must endure difficult situations that seem to threaten our hopes and dreams. These challenging moments can be painful and

MICHAEL ROSS AND TESS COX

leave us feeling lonely, frightened, and hopeless. But if you remember who you are and hold tight to the vision God has given you for your life, you will continue to move forward in the right direction. Remember, it's the trees that have a strong root system grounded deep in the earth and have the ability to bend that survive the greatest storms of life. Put down deep roots in God's love for you. Trust His Word and promises for your life.

In that process, God will also help reveal to us our weaknesses, vulnerabilities, and perhaps even some darkness that needs to be dealt with. But if we want to become the strongest persons we can be, He will work with us to become more than we ever thought we could be!

Sometimes that work is painful, but if we allow God to work in us to root out some of the darkness (that tries to hang on for dear life in our hearts), then ultimately we will become more light and less dark, more love and less fear, and more strong and less weak.

God has created great beauty and strength inside us! We must be diligent to surrender to Him as He helps us dig deep for those things, no matter how deep He has to go. It's worth it! Painful, but worth it!

Tool #3: Know what you want.

How do you find out what you want? It's a daily process

that involves constantly asking yourself how you really feel about your life, your dreams, decisions, fears, joys, loves, and talents. What do you do well? What makes you happy when you're doing it? Which subjects do you enjoy learning about in school? What interests you? The process of asking God daily to reveal truth to you will reveal the answers to the deepest desires of your heart.

Sometimes keeping a journal and writing things down can help make these things clearer.

One powerful tool to help you get a clear vision for your life is to look ahead. Imagine yourself at age twenty-six. What will your life look like? Do you have a job? Where do you live? Do you have a spouse? Children? Or are you pursuing your master's degree or PhD? Great job? Working hard? Have your own apartment, buying your own clothes, paying your own bills, and making your own decisions?

More importantly, what kind of person are you? Are you a person of integrity? Do people trust you because you have a track record for making good decisions and showing wisdom? What kind of reputation do you have in your community?

Pray about each of these things. God wants to guide you on this journey. Ask the Holy Spirit to go ahead of you and lead you down the proper path. Read your Bible and memorize scripture that will help you remember God's plan.

This is good, solid preparation for your life and relationships. Having a vision for your life will give you something to work toward and will help keep you on track when people and situations come along that are tempting to sidetrack you from your goals! All it takes is having unprotected sex *once* to become pregnant or get a disease—and completely wreck the vision of your life. At the very least, it would make it much, much harder to achieve.

More than anything, making bad decisions in the heat of the moment can lead to broken hearts and broken dreams. Don't let it happen to you. Have a plan and keep your vision strong!

Proverbs 29:18 (KJV) says, "Where there is no vision, the people perish." Do you have a vision for your life? Hold it close and keep it alive. Don't let anything (or anyone), including pressure to conform, stand in your way! Go for it!

Tool #4: Surrender your heart to Jesus.

Ask the Holy Spirit daily to teach you more about yourself and to reveal His heart and His dream for you. The inward journey is the greatest adventure of your life. Jesus loves you so much, just the way you are now. But He also loves you so much He opened the door to a future that is more interesting than anything you could ever plan! His plan is laced with unexpected twists and turns and a little mystery to spice it up. Let's face it: life never turns out exactly the way we think it will.

God's dream for you is bigger than any dream you could dream for yourself. He knows you better than you know yourself because He designed and created you. And He will reveal your own heart to you in surprising ways you cannot predict. This is a daily process and doesn't happen all at once, even though God will sometimes give you sudden inspiration and revelation—like turning on a light.

You are *not* just a sum of your appearance, sports abilities, popularity, and grades. You are an amazing creation full of surprises and strength. And God's desire is to continue the creation process inside you throughout your life. But you have to allow Him to do this. In fact, *you must invite Him to do this work of revelation in you.* It can be scary and joyful. But as wisdom comes and you begin to see yourself through God's loving eyes, you'll allow Him to reveal to you who you really are and guide you to be true to yourself, even as you are learning to be true to Him.

Tool #5: Be accountable for your thoughts and actions.

Find someone trustworthy whom you can speak to

about private thoughts, fears, and dreams. This might be a parent, a relative, or a pastor or teacher. Remember, your friends are going through the same learning process you are, so they may not have a lot of wisdom for the questions or situations you might face.

Being "accountable" means to be transparent and allow someone else to know your actions, behavior, and motivations, even some of your secrets, so they can give you honest feedback about the decisions and choices you're making. This "accountability" adult should be someone you respect and look up to, but also someone you trust not to judge you or give away your secrets.

Okay! That's a good start. What setting smart boundaries and realistic goals come down to is protecting yourself from harm and being responsible. And these things can totally be done while you are living your life. Go out, make friends, have fun, and explore your world. If you are dating, these principles of self-awareness and growth will provide a good foundation for making good decisions.

Here are some other suggestions to help you stay strong, stick to your principles, and get out of sticky situations while still maintaining your friendship/relationship with that special someone.

- Have some preplanned phrases that you will use to avoid potentially difficult physical situations. You may not be able to think straight in the moment.

- Always make sure you know where you are going and who may be joining you on the date.

- Keep your phone on you at all times. It's much easier to call or text for a rescue if you have easy access to your phone.

- When going out with someone new, make sure your date meets your parents or an adult at the beginning of the night. It's good for your date to know that someone is paying attention and cares for your safety.

- Be open about your faith and commitment to purity with your date *before* the relationship starts getting serious.

- As your relationship grows, be sure to talk with each other and set some ground rules about your expectations. This is not meant to take the romance out of your relationship but actually to eliminate a lot of anxiety.

- Pray about your relationship. Listen to God as He gives you wisdom and discernment about your relationship. Allow the Spirit to lead you. If something doesn't seem quite right, listen to that God-given intuition!

- Along that same vein, spending time with groups of people or other friends will help you stay out of situations where you are alone and temptation will be strong.

- On your first few dates, *give yourself* a curfew. That will limit the amount of alone time you have with that person.

- Have fun together. Take a cooking class, go bowling, attend one of those crazy painting classes, or try something new. Get creative!

- Talk about God. Find out if your date is comfortable talking about faith. This can give you a huge insight into where they are spiritually.

If you understand that sex is far more than just a physical act, then you are steps ahead of some of your friends. Learn as much as you can, make a plan, and take charge of your dating life. God has great things planned for you. Seek His vision for your life. He wants you to have an amazing future.

CHAPTER 10

Guilt-Free Sex, God's Way

Discover the Lord's Design for Sexual Intimacy

What if I never meet the right girl?
What if I turn out to be a failure with the opposite sex?
What if I'm destined to spend my whole life alone?
What if. . .

The questions swarmed my (Michael's) brain like an army of bloodthirsty mosquitoes then waged a war on the pit of my stomach. I was fifteen and had just been slammed hard by a very painful, very lonely, avoid-at-any-cost experience: *rejection from a girl*.

My buddy Alan had the brilliant idea of setting me up with one of our school's most popular eighth graders.

"Sheila?" I gasped. "Are you crazy? We say hi in the halls and she signed my yearbook last year—but she's not interested in *me*."

"I'm positive she likes you," Alan insisted. "I'm never wrong about these things."

Mistake #1: **I listened to a guy who claimed he was never wrong about girls.**

My buddy pointed me in her direction then convinced me that the moment was right. "She's alone. . .waiting for you to make a move," he said. "Now stop being a wimp and get yourself a girlfriend."

Mistake #2: **I let myself believe that being "girl-less" meant being less of a guy.**

I swallowed back my fear and inched my way toward Sheila. (Being a wimp seemed a lot easier—especially if I could melt into a crack on the floor.)

Mistake #3: **I tried to turn a casual friendship into something romantic—even though it wasn't right.**

Sheila flashed her unforgettable smile—the one that always turned up the speed on my heart rate.

I cleared my throat then blurted out a bunch of jumbled thoughts: "I was thinking. . . Well, Alan told me. . . What I'm trying to say is, I like you, and it would be cool if. . ."

Before I could pry loose another word from my tongue, Sheila's warm expression turned into a cold stare. And without saying a word, she walked right past me and practically decked Alan. "If Michael asks," she snarled, "*you're dead*!" She then disappeared into the girls' restroom.

Alan looked at me with a sheepish grin. "Ouch!" he said.

The last thing I remember was melting into a crack on the floor.

I survived my first big female flop and eventually learned the basics of impressing a girl—like. . .*never* stepping on cracks when I'm feeling wimpy and *always* using complete sentences when I'm attempting to communicate.

But as I grew into manhood, I discovered a frustrating fact about the male species. (Take note of this, girls.) Regardless of a boy's age or how much he's dated, he'd rather be flogged, quartered, and burned at the stake than risk rejection from the opposite sex.

I was never more aware of this than when I knelt in front of the woman I deeply love—Tiffany—and asked the ultimate question: "Will you marry me?"

It was Christmas Eve 1996, and Tiffany and I had spent the afternoon hiking in the wilderness near her parents' home in Pineville, West Virginia.

"This is my favorite spot," Tiffany said when we reached the end of the trail—a steep ridge with a postcard-perfect view. "I used to come here when I had big decisions to pray about."

"I can see why," I said. "This place definitely feels a little closer to God."

Rugged mountains and misty groves of oak and spruce stretched endlessly across the West Virginia landscape. It didn't take a bolt of lightning (or my buddy Alan) to convince me that the setting was ideal and the *moment was right*. More important, I knew that Tiffany was the *right woman*.

Asking this extraordinary woman to spend her life with me involved a risk. After all, God could have had other plans for Tiffany. Yet several key things had given me confidence:

Tiffany and I had built our relationship on a foundation of . . .

- *faith*. Jesus, and His will for our lives, was the center of our desires. He—not the status of having someone to date—defined our self-worth.

- *friendship*. We'd spent a little more than two years getting to know each other. This meant countless hours having fun together and asking each other hard questions. True intimacy always grows *slowly* out of the solid soil of "knowing" each other casually and intently.

- *support*. We kept our relationship within sight of our families. One of the first steps I took was to ask Tiffany's dad for his permission to get married, as well as his blessing on our life together.

- *sexual purity.* Nothing can ruin a relationship quicker than going too far too fast too soon. I'm proud we'd made a commitment to stay pure for each other—and for God.

I reached into my jacket pocket and pulled out a small velvet box, then handed it to Tiffany. "I have an early Christmas gift for you," I said.

She ran her finger across the lid and smiled. "I bet it's jewelry!"

As Tiffany reached in and gently pulled out a diamond engagement ring, the expression on her face gave me a solid clue to her answer. (And it was far from a cold stare!)

I knelt. "I couldn't imagine spending the rest of this life without you," I said, looking deeply into her brown eyes. "Will you marry me?"

Tiffany's smile grew even bigger. *"Yes!"*

Before we headed down the mountain to share the news with Tiffany's family, I spent some time talking to my Father: *Thank You, God, for this priceless woman You've given me. Waiting for her has been worth it. I give You this marriage. Bless it, use it, and let Your will be done.*

I'm sure that marriage is several years down the road for you, but like most guys and girls, you probably share the dream of one day spending your life with the right person. Take that dream seriously!

Don't set yourself up for a fall by forcing romantic expectations on everyone you date. Instead, build a firm foundation for your future marriage by making a commitment to seeking God's will and saving yourself for His best.

And as you grow into adulthood—and closer to finding the person of your dreams—never forget: waiting is worth it!

Discovering God's Plan for Sex and Marriage

Despite the sex-on-credit, play-now-pay-later culture we live in, not everyone is doing it. Lots of teens are saving up for good sex—when it's *really* safe and *really* right. (The kind reserved for the honeymoon and blessed by God.)

Take the thousands who have marched in the national capitals of Canada and the United States through the years, taking a stand with organizations like Liberty Counsel's "Day of Purity," LifeWay youth events, and Youth for Christ's DCLA Conferences. Proud of their virginity—and not afraid to admit it—many signed "purity pledge" cards. During one particular DCLA event several years ago, more than 210,000 of these cards were displayed in Washington, DC, and Ottawa as a visual representation of teenagers all over the world who have made a pact for purity. Yet do you catch yourself ever wondering if you're the only virgin left on the planet, and even feeling a little weird for waiting?

Let's recap some themes we've covered in this book.

Trust God's design for sex. As we shared in chapters 8 and 9 (and echoed throughout these pages), sex is designed for only one kind of committed relationship: holy matrimony. When a husband and a wife have sexual intercourse, something happens to the two of them that changes them at the deepest level. A man and a woman are bound together *body and soul.* And this bond is never supposed to be separated. (Can you see why divorce is so devastating?)

In other words, sex isn't just physical, and it's not a trivial act that feels good for a few seconds and then is over for good. Sex involves a couple's body, mind, and emotions in an activity that is intended to continue for a lifetime.

God designed our sexuality to operate within the protection and commitment of marriage. God made sex to end in full consummation. Every step along the path of pure sexuality—from an initial glance between husband and wife to a kiss, potentially leads toward physical oneness. In marriage, things are supposed to progress—things are allowed to get "out of hand."[1]

Focus on what the Bible says. Since scripture does not *specifically* say, "Don't have sex before marriage," some teens try to argue that premarital sex must be okay. (Remember our discussion in chapter 2?) Yet the Bible clearly communicates this equation:

$$premarital\ sex = sin$$

A number of passages in the Bible tell us that marriage is the right place for sex—and *specifically* state that extramarital alternatives are off-limits for believers. Take a look:

Adultery is wrong—Exodus 20:14
Sex with a prostitute is wrong—1 Corinthians 6:15–17
Impurity is wrong—Colossians 3:5–7

With verses such as these, is it possible that God would make an exception for premarital sex? Is sex outside of marriage something He considers pure and moral? Of course He doesn't.

As you set off on this whole dating, relating, waiting thing, realize that behind every handsome smile and pretty face is a person with feelings. Or to put it another way, the guy or girl you date today will probably be someone else's spouse in the future. So give your date some respect, not baggage. Remember that selfishness is a monster that can damage both people in a relationship. It's your responsibility to protect each other.

Take some advice from a "big brother." Check out the

following letter from a guy who went too far in a dating relationship—and desperately wishes he hadn't. Eighteen-year-old Sean of Grand Rapids, Michigan, sent it to me, along with a request: "Please print this so other guys and girls can hear the truth and maybe avoid the mistakes I've made."

I have something important to say to every teen guy and girl out there. I'm an eighteen-year-old who has always heard Christian views about premarital sex and the consequences of giving in. Unfortunately, I didn't listen. It seems that the whole world is telling us that sex is okay. And it is—strictly within the bonds of marriage. But instead of following God's Word, I tuned in the world and gave away my virginity.

At the time, I was convinced that having sex was the most wonderful thing in the world. Afterward, it left the girl and me with heartache. I don't mean simple hurt feelings; I'm talking about utter heartache. Not a day goes by that I don't regret that first sexual touch. Why? Because it gradually led to other things—and eventually to intercourse.

I know that God has forgiven me for my sins, but I can't help asking myself, Will my future wife forgive me? *How am I going to tell her that I gave away a gift that was meant only for her? And on my wedding night, I'll have pictures of other girls in my head, which is so wrong! To treat women as most of the secular world does is absolute sin.*

Guys, girls. . .I envy every one of you who doesn't know what sexual intimacy with a girl is like. If you're a virgin, you are so fortunate. I pray that you'll stay pure for marriage and that God will richly bless your marriage bed. And as much as you want sex now, remember that God has the right kind of woman in mind for you—that is, if it's His desire for you to be married. Hold strong and give your future wife the gift of your virginity

---

If you're convinced that marriage is in your future, take seriously this important advice: "Do not be yoked together with unbelievers. For what do righteousness and wickedness have in common? Or what fellowship can light have with darkness? . . . Or what does a believer have in common with an unbeliever?" (2 Corinthians 6:14–15 NIV). These are good questions to ask yourself.

The fact is, when two people are yoked together, they must both pull in the same direction. But by definition, Christians and non-Christians are headed in different directions. Apply this to romance and you have disaster. (The couple ends up going nowhere, and they keep rubbing sores on each other in the process.) Getting involved romantically just won't work. It's best to find a mate who says "God" a lot and knows *who* they're talking about!

CHAPTER 11

"But I've Already Blown It—What Now?"

How to De-shame Your Identity and Start Over

There. It's done. Whether planned or not, you've stepped over a big line and had sex with someone. What now? This can be a very scary thing for both guys and girls. Many times people are surprised at how unromantic and awkward their experience is. They are not left feeling "mature" and loved but rather fearful and vulnerable. An intense moment of physical attraction can be followed by intense feelings of anxiety and worry. Closeness can turn into loneliness. Pleasure can lead to pain. Your focus on a bright future can quickly change into planning for a baby or treating a sexually transmitted disease. Most people have no real idea of how many other people their sexual partner has been with. As you may already know, STDs can "hide" only to show up months or years later with devastating consequences. And no matter who gave it to *you*, it is now a part of your reality—one that you will have to explain to your future partner.

Stress

Some have compared the aftermath of having sex outside of marriage to PTSD—post-traumatic stress disorder. Some of the symptoms are difficulty falling or staying asleep, high anxiety levels, feeling jittery and worried or fearful, pulling away from close friends or family for fear they will find out, or lashing out at them and being angry all the time. On top of that, the fear of pregnancy or STDs can be a tremendous burden to bear alone.

For Christians, there is also the fear that God is now angry with them and will punish them for their sin. Some people experience guilt and shame associated with failing to live up to the standards of their faith community or the fear of being ostracized by or cast out of their faith community.

Some people may feel elated and happy while others may feel nothing at all. But most are very, very disappointed, because having sex does not actually bring them closer emotionally to someone if there's no commitment. It can leave them feeling empty and worthless and even unloved.

Now, how do they go on?

Damage Control

To be honest, we do a lot of damage to ourselves when we walk outside of God's plan for our lives or break one of

His spiritual laws. We are usually pretty harsh on ourselves and place a lot of blame on ourselves or the person with whom we've had sex.

But how does God, our heavenly Father, see us? He will never love us any less. But we know He sees our sin, and that can cause *us* to create distance in our relationship with Him. How? Because when we know we have disappointed someone we love, we tend to move away from them emotionally and distance ourselves to lessen the pain of hurting them and to ease our guilt.

God does not move away from us during times when we disobey or go astray from His plan. He understands the hurt, the shame, and the fear we experience. Jesus was also human, remember? He gets it. He gets *you*. So never believe for a minute that He is condemning you or casting you away from His presence. The Holy Spirit is surrounding you and will never leave you or forsake you. You belong to Jesus, and that will not change.

So, what can you do to make things right again?

Scars

Let's face it, once you've had sex with someone, you can't undo that. Your body is changed forever. If you've become pregnant or contracted an STD (which is quite common for teenagers who have unprotected sex), you will need medical attention right away. Some STDs are silent. You can carry them for years without knowing you have them until one day they become evident or you find out you cannot have children because of the long-term scarring or damage from the silent infection.

As Christians we believe that a living human egg uniting with a living human sperm creates a living human being, even in its tiniest form. To delete that life through abortion is a very serious thing. And that kind of act *will* leave emotional, mental, and sometimes even physical scars on you for a long time.

What if it wasn't my fault?

Unfortunately, another scary aspect of sex for many young people is that their first experience with sex is forced and not consensual. If this has happened to you, you need to tell someone, because the trauma doesn't just go away on its own. Don't let it damage your future relationships and even marriage.

A lot of emotions are hiding inside you. You may feel ashamed, guilty, or worried that you will be blamed. You may feel angry and want to lash out. This is normal, but these feelings will put you in an emotional cage and destroy you a little at a time. Some people will take matters into their own hands and try to protect themselves from further abuse. Acting out sexually, running away, or numbing the pain with alcohol or drugs can be attempts to gain control in the worst of situations. Don't let this evil have victory over you! There are many advocates who want to help you. Tell someone—a law enforcement officer, a doctor, a trusted adult, a counselor at school. Be victorious over it. Ask for help.

Keys to a Fresh Start

What about God's view of who you are now? He still loves you deeply and wants to help you get back on track. Jesus wants to heal your heart and give you a fresh start spiritually, emotionally, and mentally.

A young woman I (Tess) know who had sex at a really young age but has since renewed her relationship with Jesus had this to say: "If you are a man or a woman out there [who] has lost their virginity. . .and you're scared because you don't believe you can be pure again, just pray! Pray that God will make you pure again, because through Christ all things are possible. You are cleansed when you go to God. You are heard when you go to Him. He will forever be by your side through all the sorrow and happiness. He'll guide you out of your wrong [choices] and into right ones. God will always be there for you!"

Keys to Freedom

If you really want to live in the freedom and love of God but you know you've made bad choices, the first key to freedom is *repentance*! Come to Him, tell Him all about it. Pour your heart out to Him and tell the truth about what happened and why it happened. Then, because you know it was a sin, ask Him to forgive you and wipe the slate clean.

And guess what? He will. God will forgive and wipe the slate clean. Done. That's it. Jesus is all about second chances (and third, and fourth, and fifth. . .) because He loves you and wants to save you and help you make life-giving choices.

You may still have to face *consequences* of your former choices and actions. But you won't be running scared and all alone. If you turn to Him daily and walk with Him, He will be with you in all of it, guiding and leading you on a path of righteousness, a path that leads to truth and love and goodness. The Holy Spirit will give you strength to walk through it and be strong and do the right thing even when circumstances look their darkest. He promised never to leave us or forsake us. *Ever.*

God is not out to punish you. You know the character of God: love, forgiveness, mercy, grace, goodness, self-control, honesty, and strength. If you talk to Him and ask

Him to give you these things, then you are praying according to His will! He will be standing with you, going before you, and fighting for you each step of the way. He wants for you to succeed and for your heart to be more like His.

Repentance is the key. Being honestly sorry that you broke a law of heaven and willing to allow God to change your heart and help you change your behavior is the key to living beyond what you've done. Repentance means to turn 180 degrees and walk in the opposite direction.

Do you think this is easy? No, it isn't easy at all. But we don't have to come up with repentance all on our own. God can give it to us as a gift. If you are angry or hurt and can't think straight and don't know what to do, ask God to give you the gift of repentance so you can come to Him and allow Him to wipe your heart clean and give you a brand-new start. He loves doing that! Why? Because He wants you, He chooses you, and He has a plan for your life.

The second key is having *determination and willpower*. Whether you're a guy or a girl, the key to turning this failure into a victory is this: your willing heart. The Bible says if you seek God with all your heart (Jeremiah 29:13), you will find Him; and if you commit your plans to Him (Proverbs 16:3), we can be confident that He hears us and will give us what we ask for when we pray according to His will (1 John 5:14–15).

Ask God to give you wisdom and discernment to help you steer clear of situations that may land you in the same quagmire of shame and fear. God wants to help you run the race of life, not just limp along. He wants to clean your heart, restore your future, give you a reason and a vision for your life, and keep you walking forward into the marvelous dream He has for you.

The third key follows on after determination: *make a plan*. Figure out how or why you had sex outside of marriage, and then make a *plan* to stay out of that situation again.

Examine your heart. Ask the Holy Spirit to help you search your heart as you explore the reasons why you crossed the line. Try to remember what you were thinking and feeling at the time. Would you make the same decision today? The most common reasons why people have sex outside of marriage belong to one of these categories: desire and a longing for love, fear, or rebellion as we discussed in chapter 9. Do you fall into one of these categories?

The more self-aware you are, the better able you will be to identify those same feelings and motivations in the future. And this will help you to make better decisions moving forward. Using wisdom and discernment will help you to make more mature decisions and hopefully avoid the same mistakes.

Broken into Pieces

Previously we talked about how sex makes us "one" with the other person. And when we leave or separate from them, they take part of us with them—a part we never get back. Over time, if we have sex with many different people, *we own less and less of ourselves*, and we walk around for the rest of our lives looking for someone who can restore us to wholeness.

Only God can restore you. Only He has the power and love to re-create your heart and spiritually make you whole again. No lover, no wife or husband can fulfill this "divine" assignment to make you whole. That's why God tells us to only join ourselves to someone sexually inside a lifelong commitment of marriage: *to help keep us whole.*

Being self-aware is a lifelong journey that needs to be the foundation of your future relationships. The Holy Spirit is longing to begin that journey with you. Start today. Allow Him to re-create your spirit and your future and put the past behind you. Allow Him to walk with you if you are facing consequences of past hurt. Allow Him to put the pieces back together and restore the lost parts of your life. He loves you and doesn't want you to have to bear the burden of living with the hurt. Choose life.

CHAPTER 12

Pray *Now* for Your Future Mate

Prepare Your Heart Today for What God Has Tomorrow

Most guys and girls share the same dream: *Somewhere out there is that one person with whom I can share all of my secrets; my soul mate. . .the person God picked out just for me. Someday we'll find each other.*

That's a great life goal. And God may very well want you to be married. Then again, He may not. But as you pursue this dream, brace yourself: you'll receive all kinds of advice from well-intentioned people.

At one point in my life, when I (Tess) was especially distressed about being single, here's what an older woman told me: "Buy a pair of men's pants that would suit the kind of person you want to marry, and place them at the foot of your bed. Every night ask God to fill them!"

Apparently this worked for her but not for me. (Not yet, that is!)

A guy friend received this advice from his grandfather:

"Date a lot of girls. When you find the one who can cook well and pay her own bills, marry that one."

Like I said—they're well-intentioned people!

I have a better exercise in mind. Actually, it's more of a journey—and it's something that every guy and girl should begin during their teen years. Here's what I believe will be the best advice you'll ever receive: lay a foundation *now* for your future marriage by striving to become the person God wants you to be, which will be exactly the person your future mate will need. Honestly—do this right now. Do it well *before* you begin that search; long *before* you try to build a life with another person.

How should you begin? Take these three steps: (1) Examine your heart and your motives. (2) Define yourself and the kinds of qualities you're seeking in another person. (3) Pray for your future mate.

Examine Your Heart

Alcoholism, drug abuse, sexual addictions, greed, insecurities, depression, worry—every family struggles with something. And to be honest, we're all addicts.

"I am not being flippant when I say that all of us suffer from addiction," says expert Gerald G. May, MD. "Nor am I reducing the meaning of addiction. I mean in all truth that the psychological, neurological, and spiritual dynamics of full-fledged addiction are actively at work in every human being. The same processes that are responsible for addiction to alcohol and narcotics are also responsible for addiction to ideas, work, relationships, power, moods, fantasies, and an endless variety of other things. We are all addicts in every sense of the word."[1]

Dr. May says our addictions are our own worst enemies. They enslave us with chains of our own making, and yet they are beyond our control. "Addiction also makes idolaters of us all because it forces us to worship these objects of attachment, thereby preventing us from truly, freely loving God and one another. . . . Yet, in still another paradox, our addictions can lead us to a deep appreciation of grace. They can bring us to our knees."[2]

Amazingly, the chains of addiction can be broken in our lives.

Yet as teens grow into adulthood and young adults move into the middle years, too many of them settle into complacency, telling themselves, "These are my flaws and my shortcomings. This is who I am. My parents were this way, their parents were this way. . .and I am, too. I doubt I'll ever change."

Don't become this type of person. Instead, do the following:

- *Give Jesus full access to your heart.* A wise friend once said, "God cannot heal what you're not willing to give up." Let go—and expect your life to change as you surrender yourself to Jesus. Invite Him into the deepest regions of your heart, your spirit, and your personality.

• *Ask Jesus for strength as He reveals what needs to change within you.* If He is your guide, Jesus will gently walk you through "the fires" of fear, confusion, and heartache. . .and He will purify you.

• *Ask God to mold you into the kind of person He wants you to be.* Ask Him these key questions:
  1. What kind of a future wife or husband will I be?
  2. What do You want to heal in my life before I commit to another?
  3. In what ways do I need to grow?

Here are some additional questions that you should ponder in the weeks ahead:

• Do I feel the need to always be right?
• Do I feel the need to have the last word?
• Do I feel the need to win every argument?
• When was the last time I compromised with someone?

- Are my opinions the only ones that matter to me?
- Am I a bully?
- How flexible am I when I don't get my way? Is it my way or the highway?
- Are my plans always the best (or only) ones I will cooperate with?
- How do I handle my own anger? Do I drink? Use drugs? Yell? Hit? Withdraw?
- Do I have bad habits that might create a wedge between me and my life partner? How willing am I to get rid of those habits?
- Am I accountable for my own mistakes or bad behavior?
- What are my habitual sins? Temptations?
- What can I do to be accountable for them and turn away from them in true repentance?
- What is there in my life that would make me a poor friend, husband, or father?

Define Yourself and the Qualities That Matter to You

As you continue looking inward in prayerful reflection, consider these words from author and theologian Henri Nouwen: "To expect another human being, a mere mortal, to fulfill these 'divine' expectations is unrealistic and unfair! No human being can do for you what only

God can do!"[3] So, in the context of marriage, your future husband or wife cannot complete you and make you whole. (Sorry, Jerry Maguire, but you got that one wrong!) In fact, marriage alone cannot heal you. It's only Christ inside of a holy union that can complete us.

Marriage should be built on trust, friendship, and the willingness to "lay down your life" and compromise. In this kind of relationship, the same person doesn't always get their way all the time. If they do, that's a big red flag: perhaps one partner is manipulative or seriously immature.

It's time for more of that inward reflection. Do you pout and whine until you get your way? Do you sulk and give the silent treatment until your partner relents and gives in just to keep the peace? Is that the kind of person you want to be married to? And if you must always get your way, then you probably aren't ready for a serious relationship either. What makes you think that someone will want to marry you with that kind of personality trait? To be blunt, you need to give yourself several years to grow up. (Flip back to chapter 4 and reread the shared meaning communication exercise.)

In the spaces provided, define yourself (based on the questions you pondered above), jot down what you must work on, and define the qualities that matter most to you, as well as the ones you are looking for in another person.

I am mostly. . .

1. _____

_____

2. _____

_____

3. _____

_____

I need to change. . .

1. _____

_____

2. _____

_____

3. _____

_____

These are the character and personality qualities that matter most to me:

1. _____

_____

2. _____

_____

3. _____

_____

This is what I'm looking for in my future mate:

1. _____
   _____

2. _____
   _____

3. _____
   _____

Pray for Your Future Mate

If you make a list of attributes you are currently looking for in a forever partner, make sure you bring your list to God and literally pray over each "desirable trait" you have placed on it. Ask your Father in heaven to send you a person who can be a good helper for you in life. . .a friend beyond compare, a faithful companion provided by His very own heart for you.

How else can you pray for your future wife or husband? Try this:

Pray for their relationship with God. Begin praying for that unknown partner *now*, before you've even met them. If you desire to marry a godly man or woman, begin praying for their spirit to be open to the move and voice of the Holy Spirit. Ask God to speak to them strongly and to help them hear His voice. After all, being married to a man or woman who actually listens to God and obeys His voice means you will be able to trust them on a deeper level. Pray that they would be a man or woman of the Word, able to pray the Word of God and to receive and believe its promises.

Pray for their success. Ask God to bless them with a responsible attitude toward finances, to stay out of debt, and to save their money for the future. Ask God to give them favor at their job, to be promoted and blessed in the work of their hands.

Pray for their peace. May the Holy Spirit go before them, make their path straight, and hinder all efforts by the enemy to trip them up, bring dismay, or discouragement or despair.

Pray for their heart. Perhaps they are in another relationship right now. Pray that God will protect their heart from being wounded or abused. Ask the Holy Spirit to give them wisdom to get out of the relationship without wounding the other person.

Pray for their wisdom. Ask the Holy Spirit to speak wisdom to their heart in everything they attempt to do with their life and in their relationships with their friends, family, and coworkers.

Pray for their hopes and dreams. Ask the Lord to pour into them His dream for their life, His plans, His desires. Pray that God's desires will become their desires (pray this for yourself, too). Ask God to give them courage to step out and make some of those dreams come true and to make good decisions and choices in walking into the plans God has for them.

Each of these prayers reflect the mature desire a godly husband or wife has for their future partner. Praying for that person now will get you in the habit of doing it daily when they actually become the most important person in your life. It will also draw you closer to your heavenly Father and give the Holy Spirit access to your own desires, hopes, and dreams so He can mold and shape you into the kind of person you need to become *before* you even meet your future mate.

It's never a bad idea to share your hopes and dreams with an accountability partner who can help you pray and also give you loving, truthful feedback about your "list" and those things in your own life that may need to undergo God's creative reconstruction as you walk forward on your journey toward marriage.

So when it comes to future relationships—and eventually to marriage—save yourself from heartaches. Begin your very own prayer journey right now, asking the Lord to prepare your heart today for what He has planned for tomorrow.

God is with you. Keep your hand in His and your face turned toward Him. He will direct your path.

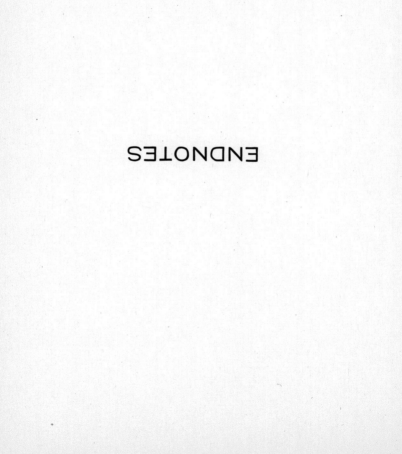

ENDNOTES

Start Here

1. Justin Lookadoo, *The Dirt on Sex* (Grand Rapids: Revell, 2004), 8.

Chapter 1. What's Your Dating DQ (Dating Quotient)?

1. This scenario was written by freelance writer Jeremy V. Jones and is adapted from Michael Ross, *BOOM: A Guy's Guide to Growing Up* (Wheaton, IL: Tyndale House, 2003), 90.

Chapter 2. Getting Ready for the Dating-Relating Thing

1. Joshua Harris, "I Kissed Dating Goodbye," *Breakaway*, February 1998, 21.

2. Adapted from "The Art of Non-Dating" by Greg Trine with Michael Ross, *Breakaway*, February 1996, 27.

Chapter 4. Mixed Signals: Guy/Girl Communication Differences

1. Freelance writer Manfred Koehler contributed to this section.

Chapter 5. Find a *Real* Person...Not a Hollywood Myth

1. Henri Nouwen, *Reaching Out, Three Spiritual Movements* (New York: Doubleday, 1975), 29–30, emphasis mine.

Chapter 7. Seven Secrets Girls Need to Know about Guys

1. Donald M. Joy, *Sex, Strength and the Secrets of Becoming a Man* (Ventura, CA: Regal, 1990), 83.

2. Adapted from Michael Ross and Susie Shellenberger, *What Your Son Isn't Telling You* (Minneapolis: Bethany House, 2010), 38.

3. Glenn Good, professor of counseling psychology at the University of Missouri-Columbia. Quotes obtained by Michael Ross through interviews conducted between 2007 and 2014.

Chapter 9. Setting Smart Boundaries and Realistic Goals with the Opposite Sex

1. Michael Ross, *Faith That Breathes* (Uhrichsville, OH: Barbour, 2006), 172.

Chapter 10. Guilt-Free Sex, God's Way

1. Joshua Harris, "I Kissed Dating Goodbye," *Breakaway*, February 1998, 21.

Chapter 12. Pray *Now* for Your Future Mate

1. Gerald G. May, MD, *Addiction and Grace* (San Francisco: HarperCollins, 1988), 3–4.

2. Ibid.

3. Henri Nouwen, *The Wounded Healer* (New York: Doubleday, 1972), x.

ABOUT THE AUTHORS

Michael Ross is an award-winning journalist and the author, coauthor, and collaborator of more than 30 books. The former editor of Breakaway, a national magazine for teen guys published by Focus on the Family, today he oversees Back to the Bible's book publishing efforts. He and his wife, Tiffany, live in Lincoln, Nebraska, with their young son, Christopher.

Tess Cox, PAC, is a writer, missionary, and a pediatric physician's assistant in Colorado with more than three decades of experience in medicine. She holds an M.A. in counseling and has written several articles for the American Academy of Pediatrics.

NOTES